175 Side Salads

175 Side Salads

Create fabulous salads and side dishes all year round with tempting, easy-to-make recipes and 200 photographs

Julia Canning

southwater

This edition is published by Southwater Books, an imprint of Anness Publishing Ltd, Hermes House, 88–89 Blackfriars Road, London SE1 8HA; tel. 020 7401 2077; fax 020 7633 9499 www.southwater.co.uk; www.annesspublishing.com

If you like the images in this book and would like to investigate using them for publishing, promotions or advertising, please visit our website www.practicalpictures.com for more information.

UK agent: The Manning Partnership Ltd; tel. 01225 478444; fax 01225 478440; sales@manning-partnership.co.uk

UK distributor: Grantham Book Services Ltd; tel. 01476 541080; fax 01476 541061; orders@gbs.tbs-ltd.co.uk

North American agent/distributor: National Book Network; tel. 301 459 3366; fax 301 429 5746; www.nbnbooks.com

Australian agent/distributor: Pan Macmillan Australia; tel. 1300 135 113; fax 1300 135 103; customer.service@macmillan.com.au

New Zealand agent/distributor: David Bateman Ltd; tel. (09) 415 7664; fax (09) 415 8892

ETHICAL TRADING POLICY
At Anness Publishing we believe that business should be conducted in an ethical and ecologically sustainable way, with respect for the environment and a proper regard to the replacement of the natural resources we employ. As a publisher, we use a lot of wood pulp to make high-quality paper for printing, and that wood commonly comes from spruce trees. We are therefore currently growing more than 750,000 trees in three Scottish forest plantations: Berrymoss (130 hectares/320 acres), West Touxhill (125 hectares/305 acres) and Deveron Forest (75 hectares/185 acres). The forests we manage contain more than 3.5 times the number of trees employed each year in making paper for the books we manufacture.

Because of this ongoing ecological investment programme, you, as our customer, can have the pleasure and reassurance of knowing that a tree is being cultivated on your behalf to naturally replace the materials used to make the book you are holding.

Our forestry programme is run in accordance with the UK Woodland Assurance Scheme (UKWAS) and will be certified by the internationally recognized Forest Stewardship Council (FSC). The FSC is a non-government organization dedicated to promoting responsible management of the world's forests. Certification ensures forests are managed in an environmentally sustainable and socially responsible way. For further information about this scheme, go to www.annesspublishing.com/trees

Publisher: Joanna Lorenz
Editorial Director: Helen Sudell
Project Editor: Rosie Gordon
Jacket Design: Nigel Partridge
Production Controller: Don Campaniello

Notes
Bracketed terms are intended for American readers.

For all recipes, quantities are given in both metric and imperial measures and, where appropriate, in standard cups and spoons. Follow one set of measures, but not a mixture, because they are not interchangeable.

Standard spoon and cup measures are level.
1 tsp = 5ml, 1 tbsp = 15ml, 1 cup = 250ml/8fl oz

Australian standard tablespoons are 20ml.
Australian readers should use 3 tsp in place of 1 tbsp for measuring small quantities.

American pints are 16fl oz/2 cups. American readers should use 20fl oz/2.5 cups in place of 1 pint when measuring liquids.

Electric oven temperatures in this book are for conventional ovens. When using a fan oven, the temperature will probably need to be reduced by about 10–20°C/20–40°F. Since ovens vary, you should check with your manufacturer's instruction book for guidance.

The nutritional analysis given for each recipe is calculated per portion (i.e. serving or item), unless otherwise stated. If the recipe gives a range, such as Serves 4–6, then the nutritional analysis will be for the smaller portion size, i.e. 6 servings. Measurements for sodium do not include salt added to taste.

Medium (US large) eggs are used unless otherwise stated.

Main front cover image shows Assorted Seaweed Salad – for recipe, see page 12.

Contents

Introduction

Whatever the season, or the weather, a side salad brings colour to your table and makes a healthy and delicious addition to any mealtime. From a barbecue or roast to a mid-week curry, all will be lifted by an appetizing, fresh and colourful side dish.

Because salads are almost inevitably based on fresh produce, they are more ingredient-driven than other dishes. It is no use planning to serve a superb salad, only to discover that the central ingredient is out of season, or looks limp and unappetizing. It makes sense, therefore, to abandon the usual practice of basing a meal around specific recipes before going shopping. Instead, check out what's freshest and best, and then plan your menu. Farm shops and farmers' markets are a great source of seasonal vegetables and fruits, or you may belong to a box scheme, and have a regular delivery of freshly pulled or picked produce. You may even grow your own. You don't have to own a vegetable garden to have a regular supply of fresh vegetables – seed manufacturers increasingly offer packs that are perfect for growing in pots. The range is quite extensive and includes salad leaves, rocket (arugula), chillies, bush courgettes (zucchini),

Tossing together tender pasta and roasted vegetables makes a balanced side dish, perfect with barbecued meat or fish. Fresh herbs add a wonderful flavour.

Side salads from all over the world are featured, such as this pretty, Thai-inspired sweet and sour cucumber dish, perfect for cooling down spicy meals.

dwarf beans, spring onions (scallions), carrots, sweet (bell) peppers, tomatoes and herbs of all sorts, from French tarragon to Thai basil.

This book is organized so that similar vegetables are grouped together in various categories, so whatever is in season, whether it be Jersey potatoes, glossy tomatoes or baby broad (fava) beans, you'll find it easy to locate a suitable recipe. In fact, you'll be spoiled for choice, since there are several different suggestions for many of the ingredients.

While it might be tempting to buy bags of ready-cut carrots or pre-packed salads, the recipes in this book are fresher, more economical, healthier and taste infinitely better. Many of them are also quick – taking a matter of minutes to prepare – or can be made in advance for easy lunches and healthy snacks.

Thanks to international trade, we can also use freshly-picked vegetables and fruits from far-flung countries, not to mention a huge repertoire of exotic herbs, spices and cooking methods. This means that it's possible to sample a different salad or vegetable dish every day of the year, for an exciting and healthy diet. For example, you will find that this collection offers plenty of salads to complement your favourite curry or Mexican dish, such as the grape-filled Yogurt Salad or Black Bean Salsa. Every country has its own favourite salad and it is fascinating to see how many ways there are of presenting the same ingredient. Take something as simple as a tomato, for instance. In Italy it might be mixed with bread and anchovies to make Panzanella. An Israeli cook might combine tomatoes and peppers, while in Turkey and Greece, feta cheese and black olives are popular additions. A favourite Mexican treatment is to use tomatoes in all sorts of spicy and colourful salsas, sometimes with the chillies that are so common in that country, but also with oranges and chives, coriander (cilantro) or other fresh herbs. Tomato salads can also include grains, like couscous or bulgur wheat, and are great blended with pasta or rice.

Warm salads are becoming increasingly popular, and this book contains a superb selection. Try Green Beans with Almond Butter, Roast Mediterranean Vegetables with Pecorino, or Warm Halloumi and Fennel Salad. Among the more unusual offerings are Baked Sweet Potato Salad and Stir-fried Pineapple Salad with Ginger and Chilli.

The golden rule when making a salad is to choose a few good, seasonal ingredients with complementary or contrasting textures and compatible flavours. Vegetables or fruits will provide plenty of colour, but you can also add edible flowers such as nasturtiums, marigolds or borage to brighten up a simple salad of selected green leaves.

Guacamole is just one of the salsa-type side dishes featured in this book. Salsas make delicious dips as well us colourful, healthy vegetable dishes.

Rice salads, hot and cold, are popular with children and adults alike, and can be packed full of flavour and colour – perfect for eating with seafood.

Use herbs with discretion: rocket gives green salads a lovely peppery flavour, but tastes best when balanced with milder green leaves or with a sweet fruit such as pears or figs. Parsley, dill, mint and basil all make good additions when matched with other flavours. They are easy to grow in pots, so you can get the best, fresh flavour.

Occasionally, a recipe will suggest marinating, or steeping in a dressing to allow flavours to blend, but it is more usual to add a dressing just before serving. Salad servers can be used for mixing, but many cooks prefer to use clean hands, since they are softer and less likely to bruise delicate leaves. Use only enough dressing to gloss the ingredients, enhancing their flavour without being too dominant.

The recipes in this book come with carefully selected dressings, but by mixing and matching, you can create new and different combinations, giving you even more choice when serving these versatile dishes. With practice, you will instinctively know the flavours and textures that work together.

Finally, all of these recipes have been analyzed by a nutritionist, and the energy, fat, carbohydrate and protein count, and levels of fibre, calcium and sodium, are detailed under each recipe entry. This at-a-glance information enables you to plan meals that are as balanced and nutritious as they are delicious.

Wild Rocket & Cos Lettuce Salad with Herbs

This leafy Greek-style salad combines cos lettuce, which is native to Greece, with peppery rocket and fresh herbs, producing a clean-tasting side dish. If cos lettuce is not available, romaine lettuce can be used with just as much success.

Serves 4

a large handful of rocket
    (arugula) leaves
2 cos or romaine lettuce hearts
3 or 4 fresh flat leaf parsley
    sprigs, coarsely chopped
30–45ml/2–3 tbsp finely
    chopped fresh dill
75ml/5 tbsp extra-virgin olive oil
15–30ml/1–2 tbsp lemon juice
salt

1 If the rocket leaves are young and tender they can be left whole, but older ones should be trimmed of thick stalks and then sliced coarsely. Discard any tough stalks.

2 Slice the cos or romaine lettuce hearts into thin ribbons and place these in a bowl, then add the rocket and the chopped fresh parsley and dill.

3 To make the dressing, whisk the extra-virgin olive oil and lemon juice with salt to taste in a bowl until the mixture emulsifies and thickens.

4 Just before serving, pour the dressing over the salad and toss lightly to coat the ingredients well. Serve immediately.

> **Cook's Tips**
> • It is important to balance the bitterness of the rocket and the sweetness of the cos or romaine lettuce, and the best way to find this out is by taste.
> • If you want to make the salad a little more substantial, try adding shavings of Parmesan cheese, canned anchovy fillets or steamed asparagus spears.

Mixed Green Leaf & Herb Salad

Bursting with fresh, herby flavours, this attractive salad makes an ideal side dish to serve with grilled meat or fish. You can vary the herbs according to taste and season. Try adding edible flowers, such as nasturtiums, for a splash of colour.

Serves 4

15g/½oz/½ cup mixed fresh
    herbs, such as chervil, tarragon
    (use sparingly), dill, basil,
    marjoram (use sparingly), flat
leaf parsley, mint, sorrel, fennel
    and coriander (cilantro)
350g/12oz mixed salad leaves,
    such as rocket (arugula),
    radicchio, chicory (Belgian
    endive), watercress, frisée, baby
    spinach, oakleaf lettuce
    and dandelion

For the dressing

50ml/2fl oz/¼ cup extra-virgin
    olive oil
15ml/1 tbsp cider vinegar
salt and ground black pepper

1 Wash and dry the herbs and salad leaves in a salad spinner, or use two clean, dry dish towels to pat them dry.

2 To make the dressing, whisk together the olive oil and cider vinegar in a small bowl and season with salt and pepper.

3 Place the mixed herbs and salad leaves in a large salad bowl. Just before serving, pour over the dressing and toss thoroughly with your hands to mix well. Serve immediately.

> **Cook's Tip**
> Try to get the herb and salad leaves as dry as possible otherwise the dressing will not coat properly.

> **Variation**
> To make a more substantial salad for a light lunch or supper, add baby broad (fava) beans, cooked, sliced artichoke hearts and quartered hard-boiled (hard-cooked) eggs.

Wild rocket & cos lettuce salad: Energy 135kcal/554kJ; Protein 0.6g; Carbohydrate 1.3g, of which sugars 1.3g; Fat 14.1g, of which saturates 2.1g; Cholesterol 0mg; Calcium 21mg; Fibre 0.7g; Sodium 2mg
Mixed green leaf & herb salad: Energy 88kcal/362kJ; Protein 0.8g; Carbohydrate 1.6g, of which sugars 1.6g; Fat 8.7g, of which saturates 1.3g; Cholesterol 0mg; Calcium 32mg; Fibre 1g; Sodium 4mg

Rocket & Coriander Salad

A quick and easy side salad, packed with peppery flavour.

Serves 4

115g/4oz rocket (arugula)
115g/4oz young spinach leaves
1 large bunch fresh coriander
   (cilantro), about 25g/1oz
2–3 fresh parsley sprigs

For the dressing

1 garlic clove, crushed
45ml/3 tbsp olive oil
10ml/2 tsp white wine vinegar
pinch of paprika
cayenne pepper
salt

1 Place the rocket and spinach leaves in a salad bowl. Chop the coriander and parsley and scatter them over the top.

2 Whisk together the garlic, olive oil, vinegar and paprika in a small bowl, adding cayenne pepper and salt to taste. Pour the dressing over the salad and serve immediately.

Garlicky Green Salad with Raspberry Dressing

Adding a splash of raspberry vinegar to the dressing enlivens a simple green salad, turning it into a sophisticated side dish.

Serves 4

45ml/3 tbsp olive oil
2 garlic cloves, finely sliced
4 handfuls of salad leaves
15ml/1 tbsp raspberry vinegar
salt and ground black pepper

1 Heat the oil in a small pan and add the garlic. Fry gently for 1–2 minutes, or until just golden: do not burn the garlic.

2 Remove the garlic with a slotted spoon and drain on kitchen paper. Pour the oil into a small bowl.

3 Arrange the salad leaves in a serving bowl. Whisk the vinegar into the reserved oil and season with salt and pepper. Pour the dressing over the salad, toss and sprinkle with the fried garlic.

Mixed Leaf & Herb Salad with Toasted Seeds

This simple salad is the perfect antidote to a rich, heavy meal as it contains fresh herbs that can aid the digestion.

Serves 4

115g/4oz/4 cups mixed
   salad leaves
50g/2oz/2 cups mixed salad
   herbs, such as coriander
   (cilantro), parsley, basil
   and rocket

25g/1oz/2 tbsp pumpkin seeds
25g/1oz/2 tbsp sunflower seeds

For the dressing

60ml/4 tbsp extra-virgin olive oil
15ml/1 tbsp balsamic vinegar
2.5ml/½ tsp Dijon mustard
salt and ground black pepper

1 Start by making the dressing. Combine the olive oil, balsamic vinegar and mustard in a screw-top jar. Add salt and pepper to taste. Close the jar tightly, then shake the dressing vigorously.

2 Place the salad and herb leaves in a large salad bowl and toss lightly together.

3 Toast the pumpkin and sunflower seeds in a dry frying pan over a medium heat for 2 minutes, until golden, tossing frequently to prevent them from burning. Allow the seeds to cool slightly before sprinkling over the salad.

4 Pour the dressing over the salad and toss gently with your hands until the leaves are well coated. Serve immediately.

Variations
• Balsamic vinegar adds a rich, sweet taste to the dressing, but red or white wine vinegar could be used instead.
• A few nasturtium flowers would look very pretty in this salad, as would borage flowers.

Rocket & coriander Salad: Energy 68kcal/280kJ; Protein 2g; Carbohydrate 1.3g, of which sugars 1.2g; Fat 6.1g, of which saturates 0.9g; Cholesterol 0mg; Calcium 123mg; Fibre 1.8g; Sodium 85mg
Garlicky green salad: Energy 78kcal/320kJ; Protein 0.2g; Carbohydrate 0.4g, of which sugars 0.4g; Fat 8.4g, of which saturates 1.2g; Cholesterol 0mg; Calcium 7mg; Fibre 0.2g; Sodium 1mg
Mixed lead & herb salad: Energy 178kcal/737kJ; Protein 2.9g; Carbohydrate 3.1g, or which sugars, 1g; Fat: 17.2g, or which saturates 2.2g; Cholesterol 0mg; Caclium 26mg; Fibre 1.1g; Sodium 20mg

Lettuce & Herb Salad

Shops now sell many different types of lettuce leaves all year, so try to use a mixture. Pre-packed bags of mixed baby lettuce leaves are a convenient option.

Serves 4
$^1\!/_2$ cucumber
mixed lettuce leaves
1 bunch watercress, about 115g/4oz
1 chicory (Belgian endive) head, sliced
45ml/3 tbsp chopped fresh herbs such as parsley, thyme, tarragon, chives, chervil

For the dressing
15ml/1 tbsp white wine vinegar
5ml/1 tsp Dijon mustard
75ml/5 tbsp extra-virgin olive oil
salt and ground black pepper

1 To make the dressing, mix the vinegar and mustard together, then whisk in the oil, seasoning with salt and pepper to taste.

2 Peel the cucumber, if liked, then halve it lengthwise and scoop out the seeds. Thinly slice the flesh. Tear the lettuce leaves into bitesize pieces.

3 Either toss the cucumber, lettuce, watercress, chicory and herbs together in a bowl, or arrange them in the bowl in layers.

4 Stir the dressing, then pour over the salad and toss lightly to coat well. Serve immediately.

Flower Garden Salad

Dress a colourful mixture of salad leaves with good olive oil and freshly squeezed lemon juice, then top it with crispy bread crostini.

Serves 4–6
3 thick slices day-old bread, such as ciabatta
120ml/4fl oz/$^1\!/_2$ cup extra-virgin olive oil
1 garlic clove, halved
$^1\!/_2$ small cos or romaine lettuce
$^1\!/_2$ small oakleaf lettuce
25g/1oz rocket (arugula) leaves
25g/1oz fresh flat leaf parsley
a small handful of young dandelion leaves
juice of 1 lemon
a few nasturtium leaves and flowers
pansy and pot marigold flowers
sea salt flakes and ground black pepper

1 Cut the slices of bread into 1cm/$^1\!/_2$in cubes.

2 Heat half the oil gently in a frying pan and fry the bread cubes in it, tossing them until they are well coated and lightly browned. Remove and cool.

3 Rub the inside of a large salad bowl with the cut sides of the garlic clove, then discard. Pour the remaining oil into the bottom of the bowl.

4 Tear all the salad leaves into bitesize pieces and pile them into the bowl with the oil. Season with salt and pepper. Cover and chill until you are ready to serve the salad.

5 To serve, toss the leaves in the oil at the bottom of the bowl, then sprinkle with the lemon juice and toss again. Scatter the crostini and the flowers over the top and serve immediately.

Cook's Tip
It's fun to grow your own edible flowers for salads – you can even cultivate them in a box on a window sill. If you grow your own, you can be sure that they are totally organic.

Lettuce & herb salad: Energy 1483kcal/6098kJ; Protein 0.6g; Carbohydrate 1.7g, of which sugars 1.1g; Fat 164g, of which saturates 23.5g; Cholesterol 0mg; Calcium 19mg; Fibre 0.6g; Sodium 39mg
Flower garden salad: Energy 174kcal/722kJ; Protein 2.4g; Carbohydrate 11.3g, of which sugars 1.5g; Fat 13.5g, of which saturates 2g; Cholesterol 0mg; Calcium 38mg; Fibre 0.9g; Sodium 109mg

Fresh Spinach & Avocado Salad

Young, tender spinach leaves make a change from lettuce. They are delicious served with avocado, cherry tomatoes and radishes in an unusual tofu sauce.

Serves 2–3
1 large avocado
juice of 1 lime
225g/8oz baby spinach leaves
115g/4oz cherry tomatoes
4 spring onions (scallions), sliced
½ cucumber
50g/2oz radishes, sliced

For the dressing
115g/4oz soft silken tofu
45ml/3 tbsp milk
10ml/2 tsp mustard
2.5ml/½ tsp white wine vinegar
cayenne pepper
salt and ground black pepper
radish roses and fresh herb sprigs,
   to garnish

1 Cut the avocado in half, remove the stone (pit) and strip off the skin. Cut the flesh into slices. Transfer to a plate, drizzle over the lime juice and set aside.

2 Put the baby spinach leaves in a mixing bowl. Cut the larger cherry tomatoes in half and add all the tomatoes to the mixing bowl with the spring onions. Cut the cucumber into chunks and add to the bowl with the sliced radishes.

3 To make the dressing, put the tofu, milk, mustard, vinegar and a pinch of cayenne in a food processor or blender. Add salt and pepper to taste. Process for 30 seconds, until smooth. Scrape the dressing into a bowl and add a little extra milk if you like a thinner dressing.

4 Sprinkle the dressing with a little extra cayenne and garnish with radish roses and herb sprigs. Transfer the avocado with the spinach salad to a serving dish and serve with the dressing.

Cook's Tip
Use soft silken tofu rather than the firm block variety. It can be found in most supermarkets in long-life cartons.

Vitality Salad

This colourful salad is particularly healthy and uses borage and marigold flowers and fresh herbs.

borage flowers
pot marigold petals
vinaigrette dressing, to serve

Serves 4
1 yellow (bell) pepper
mixed salad leaves: dandelion,
   baby spinach, rocket (arugula),
   lamb's lettuce (corn salad),
small bunch of mint
a few lemon balm leaves

1 Slice the pepper and mix it with the salad leaves in a large bowl. Snip in the mint and lemon balm, and top with borage flowers and marigold petals.

2 Toss the salad gently in your favourite vinaigrette dressing just before serving.

Spinach & Mushroom Salad

This nutritious salad goes well with strongly flavoured dishes. If served alone as a light lunch, it could be dressed with a French vinaigrette and served with warm, crusty French bread.

Serves 4
10 baby corn cobs
2 tomatoes
115g/4oz/1½ cups mushrooms
1 onion cut into rings
20 small spinach leaves
25g/1oz salad cress (optional)
salt and ground black pepper

1 Halve the baby corn cobs lengthwise and slice the tomatoes.

2 Trim the mushrooms and cut them into thin slices.

3 Arrange all the salad ingredients attractively in a large bowl. Season with salt and pepper and serve.

Spinach & avocado salad: Energy 137kcal/566kJ; Protein 7.5g; Carbohydrate 5.5g, of which sugars 4.7g; Fat 9.4g, of which saturates 1.9g; Cholesterol 1mg; Calcium 364mg; Fibre 3.6g; Sodium 221mg
Vitality salad: Energy 1483kcal/6098kJ; Protein 0.6g; Carbohydrate 1.7g, of which sugars 1.1g; Fat 164g, of which saturates 23.5g; Cholesterol 0mg; Calcium 19mg; Fibre 0.9g; Sodium 39mg
Spinach and mushroom salad: Energy 21kcal/89kJ; Protein 2g; Carbohydrate 2.4g, of which sugars 2.2g; Fat 0.5g, of which saturates 0.1g; Cholesterol 0mg; Calcium 29mg; Fibre 1.5g; Sodium 309mg

Sweet-and-sour Cucumber Salad

Cucumbers are sliced and dressed Thai-style with lime and herbs to make a delightful accompaniment to meat, poultry and seafood dishes. This salad is also a great addition to a summer barbecue or salad table.

Serves 4–6
2 cucumbers
30ml/2 tbsp sugar
100ml/3½fl oz/scant ½ cup
   rice wine vinegar
juice of half a lime
1–2 green Thai chillies, seeded
   and finely sliced
2 shallots, halved and finely sliced
1 small bunch each fresh
   coriander (cilantro) and
   mint, stalks removed, leaves
   roughly chopped
salt

1 Use a vegetable peeler to remove strips of the cucumber peel. Remove it all or make a striped pattern, as preferred. Halve the cucumber lengthwise and cut into slices.

2 Place the slices on a plate and sprinkle with a little salt. Leave to stand for 15 minutes, then rinse and drain.

3 In a bowl, mix the sugar with the vinegar until it has dissolved, then stir in the lime juice and a little salt to taste.

4 Add the chillies, shallots, herbs and cucumber to the dressing and leave to stand for 15–20 minutes before serving.

Assorted Seaweed Salad

Seaweed is a nutritions, alkaline food, which is rich in fibre. Its flavours are a great complement to oriental fish and tofu dishes.

Serves 4
5g/⅛oz each dried wakame,
   dried arame and dried
   hjiki seaweeds
about 130g/4½oz fresh
   enokitake mushrooms
50ml/1 tbsp rice vinegar
6.5ml/1¼ tsp salt
2 spring onions (scallions)
   a few ice cubes
½ cucumber, cut lengthwise
250g/9oz mixed salad leaves

For the dressing
60ml/4 tbsp rice vinegar
7.5ml/1½ tsp toasted sesame oil
15ml/1 tbsp shoyu
15ml/1 tbsp water with a pinch
   of dashi powder
2.5cm/1in piece fresh root ginger,
   finely grated (shredded)

1 Soak the dried wakame seaweed for 10 minutes in one bowl of water and, in a seperate bowl of water, soak the dried arame and hijiki seaweeds together for 30 minutes.

2 Trim the hard end of the enokitake mushroom stalks, then cut the bunch in half and separate the stems.

3 Cook the wakame and enokitake in boiling water for 2 minutes, then add the arame and hijiki for a few seconds. Immediately remove from the heat. Drain in a sieve (strainer) and sprinkle with the vinegar and salt while still warm. Chill.

4 Slice the spring onions (scallions) into thin, 4cm/1½in long strips, then soak the strips in a bowl of cold water with a few ice cubes added to make them curl up. Drain. Slice the cucumber into thin half-moon shapes.

5 Mix the dressing ingredients together. Arrange the mixed salad leaves with the cucumber on top, then add the seaweed and enokitake mixutre.

6 Decorate the salad with spring onion curls and serve with the dressing.

Sweet-and-sour cucumber: Energy 59kcal/248kJ; Protein 2g; Carbohydrate 12g, of which sugars 11g Fat 0g, of which saturates 0g; Cholesterol 0mg; Cacium 63mg; Fibre 0.8g; Sodium 0.2g
Assorted seaweed salad: Energy 26kcal/107kJ; Protein 1.5g; Carbohydrate 2.2g, of which sugars 2g; Fat 1.3g, of which saturates 0.2g; Cholesterol 0mg; Calcium 28mg; Fibre 1.2g; Sodium 272mg

Vegetable and Coconut Salad

This Indonesian salad is typically served to complement snacks of rice, meat or fish at street food stalls, often wrapped in a banana leaf.

Serves 4–6
225g/8oz green beans, cut into bitesize pieces
3–4 tomatoes, skinned, seeded and cut into bitesize chunks
4–6 spring onions (scallions), sliced

225g/8oz beansprouts
½ fresh coconut, grated

For the dressing
1–2 fresh red or green chillies, seeded and chopped
2 garlic cloves, chopped
25g/1oz galangal or fresh root ginger, grated
5–10ml/1–2 tsp terasi (Indonesian shrimp paste)
juice of 2–3 limes
salt and ground black pepper

1 To make the dressing, using a mortar and pestle, grind the chillies, garlic and galangal to a paste.

2 Add the terasi and juice of 2 limes. If the limes are not juicy, then squeeze the juice of the extra lime and add to the dressing, or add a little water, so that it is of pouring consistency. Season the dressing with salt and pepper to taste.

3 Put the green beans, tomatoes, spring onions, beansprouts and grated coconut into a large bowl. Using your fingers or two spoons, mix the ingredients together thoroughly.

4 Toss the dressing into the salad with clean hands, transfer to a clean bowl and serve immediately.

Cook's tip
Galangal is similar to ginger and usually sold in Asian food stores or large supermarkets. Although the two roots taste and look alike, galangal is more aromatic than ginger, and its skin is smoother, with pinkish rings.

Panzanella

Open-textured, Italian-style bread is essential for this colourful Tuscan salad.

Serves 6
10 thick slices day-old Italian style bread, about 275g/10oz
1 cucumber, peeled and cut into chunks
5 tomatoes, seeded and diced

1 large red onion, chopped
175g/6oz/1½ cups pitted black or green olives
20 fresh basil leaves, torn

For the dressing
60ml/4 tbsp extra-virgin olive oil
15ml/1 tbsp red or white wine vinegar
salt and ground black pepper

1 Soak the bread in water for 2 minutes, then squeeze it gently, with your hands, then in a dish towel to remove excess water.

2 Whisk the oil, vinegar and seasoning together. Mix the cucumber, tomatoes, onion and olives in a bowl.

3 Break the bread into chunks and add to the bowl with the basil. Pour the dressing over the salad, and toss before serving.

Variation
If your olives are preserved in a good oil, you could use this instead of the 4 tbsp extra virgin olive oil for extra flavour.

Vegetable and coconut salad: Energy 141kcal/584kJ; Protein 4.5g; Carbohydrate 6.4g, of which sugars 5.1g; Fat 11g, of which saturates 9.1g; Cholesterol 8mg; Calcium 54mg; Fibre 4.6g; Sodium 86mg
Panzanella: Energy 239kcal/1003kJ; Protein 5.5g; Carbohydrate 29.6g, of which sugars 7.1g; Fat 11.8g, of which saturates 1.6g; Cholesterol 0mg; Calcium 93mg; Fibre 3.3g; Sodium 905mg

Marinated Cucumber Salad

This wonderfully cooling salad makes a welcome addition to a summery cold spread. The cider marinade imparts a delicious flavour to the sliced cucumber, and the dill topping is the perfect finishing touch.

Serves 4-6
2 cucumbers
15ml/1 tbsp salt
90g/3½oz/½ cup sugar
175ml/6fl oz/¾ cup dry cider
15ml/1 tbsp cider vinegar
45ml/3 tbsp chopped fresh dill
ground black pepper

1 Slice the cucumbers thinly and place them in a colander, sprinkling salt between each layer. Put the colander over a bowl and leave to drain for 1 hour.

2 Thoroughly rinse the cucumber under cold running water to remove excess salt, then pat dry with kitchen paper.

3 Gently heat the sugar, cider and vinegar in a pan, until the sugar has dissolved. Remove from the heat and leave to cool. Put the cucumber slices in a bowl, pour over the cider mixture and leave to marinate for 2 hours.

4 Drain the cucumber and sprinkle with the chopped dill and black pepper to taste. Mix well and transfer to a serving dish. Chill until ready to serve.

Tofu & Cucumber Salad

A nutritious and refreshing salad with a hot, sweet-and-sour dressing, this is ideal for buffets.

Serves 4–6
1 small cucumber
115g/4oz square tofu
oil, for frying
115g/4oz/½ cup beansprouts
salt
celery leaves, to garnish

For the dressing
1 small onion, grated (shredded)
2 garlic cloves, crushed
5–7.5ml/1–1½ tsp chilli sauce
30–45ml/2–3 tbsp dark
  soy sauce
15–30ml/1–2 tbsp rice
  wine vinegar
10ml/2 tsp dark brown sugar

1 Cut the cucumber into neat cubes. Place in a colander and sprinkle with salt to extract excess liquid. Put the colander over a bowl and leave to drain for 1 hour, while you prepare the remaining ingredients.

2 Cut the tofu into cubes. Heat a little oil in a pan and fry the tofu on both sides until golden brown. Drain on kitchen paper.

3 To make the dressing, place the onion, garlic and chilli sauce in a screw-top jar. Close the jar tightly, then shake vigorously to mix. Add the soy sauce, vinegar and sugar with salt to taste. Shake the jar again until the ingredients are well combined.

4 Just before serving, rinse the cucumber under cold running water. Drain and thoroughly pat dry with kitchen paper.

5 Toss the cucumber, tofu and beansprouts together in a serving bowl and pour over the dressing. Garnish with celery leaves and serve the salad immediately.

Cook's Tip
Tofu is made from soya beans and is a good source of protein for vegetarians. It is bland tasting so needs a flavourful dressing.

Marinated cucumber salad: Energy 79kcal/335kJ; Protein 0.8g; Carbohydrate 17.7g, of which sugars 17.6g; Fat 0.2g, of which saturates 0g; Cholesterol 0mg; Calcium 39mg; Fibre 0.8g; Sodium 8mg
Tofu & cucumber salad: Energy 52kcal/215kJ; Protein 2.6g; Carbohydrate 4.3g, of which sugars 3.6g; Fat 2.8g, of which saturates 0.3g; Cholesterol 0mg; Calcium 109mg; Fibre 0.5g; Sodium 537mg

Tricolore Salad

This is a great addition to a picnic and can be served as a starter, or as a side salad to go perfectly with cold Italian meats or a creamy pasta dish.

Makes 4–6
1 small red onion, thinly sliced
6 large full-flavoured tomatoes

extra-virgin olive oil, to sprinkle
50g/2oz rocket (arugula) or watercress leaves, roughly chopped
30ml/6oz Mozzerella cheese, thinly sliced or grated
30ml/2tbsp pine nuts (otional)
salt and ground black pepper

1 Soak the onion in a bowl of cold water for 30 minutes, then drain and pat dry. Cut a cross in each tomato's skin and plunge into boiling water for 30 seconds: the skins will then slip off.

2 Slice the tomatoes and arrange half on a large platter. Sprinkle liberally with olive oil and layer on the chopped rocket or watercress, onion slices, cheese and the rest of the tomatoes, sprinkling over more oil and seasoning well between each layer. Finish with a scattering of pine nuts. These taste best if they are lightly toasted.

Sweet Cucumber Cooler

This sweet dipping sauce is good served with Thai bites.

Makes 120ml/4fl oz/¹⁄₂ cup
¹⁄₄ small cucumber, thinly sliced
75ml/5 tbsp water

30ml/2 tbsp sugar
2.5ml/¹⁄₂ tsp salt
15ml/1 tbsp rice or white wine vinegar
2 shallots or 1 small red onion, thinly sliced

1 With a sharp knife, cut the cucumber slices into quarters.

2 Measure the water, sugar, salt and vinegar into a stainless steel or enamel pan, bring to the boil and simmer for less than 1 minute until the sugar has dissolved. Allow to cool. Add the cucumber and shallots. Serve at room temperature.

Cucumber & Dill Salad

Aromatic dill is a particularly useful herb to use with salads. Here, its aniseed flavour is partnered with fresh-tasting cucumber in a soured cream dressing.

Serves 4
2 cucumbers
5ml/1 tsp salt
5 fresh dill sprigs
15ml/1 tbsp white wine vinegar
150ml/¹⁄₄ pint/²⁄₃ cup soured cream
ground black pepper

1 Use a cannelle knife (zester) to peel away strips of rind from along the length of the cucumbers, creating a striped effect. Slice thinly.

2 Put the slices in a colander and sprinkle with salt. Place the colander over a bowl and leave for to drain for 1 hour.

3 Rinse under cold water, then pat dry with kitchen paper.

4 Finely chop about 45ml/3 tbsp fresh dill, setting aside one sprig for the garnish. Put the slices of cucumber in a bowl, add the chopped dill and combine the ingredients together, either mixing with your hands or with a fork.

5 In another bowl, stir the vinegar into the soured cream and season the mixture with pepper.

6 Pour the soured cream over the cucumber and chill for 1 hour before turning into a serving dish. Garnish with the reserved sprig of dill, and serve immediately.

Cook's Tips
• Salting the cucumber draws out some of the moisture, thereby making it firmer. Make sure you rinse it thoroughly before using or the salad will be too salty.
• A cannelle knife is easy to use and is also useful for creating an attractive edge to lemon slices.

Tricolore salad: Energy 261kcal/1080kJ; Protein 11.2g; Carbohydrate 3.1g, of which sugars 3.1g; Fat 22.7g, of which saturates 9.4g; Cholesterol 33mg; Calcium 211mg; Fibre 1g; Sodium 231mg
Cucumber cooler: Energy 147kcal/624kJ; Protein 1.4g; Carbohydrate 37.2g, of which sugars 35.8g; Fat 0.2g, of which saturates 0g; Cholesterol 0mg; Calcium 44mg; Fibre 1.3g; Sodium 6mg
Cucumber & dill salad: Energy 91kcal/375kJ; Protein 2.2g; Carbohydrate 3.3g, of which sugars 3.1g; Fat 7.7g, of which saturates 4.7g; Cholesterol 23mg; Calcium 78mg; Fibre 1.2g; Sodium 23mg

Cucumber & Tomato Salad

Yogurt cools the dressing for this salad; fresh chilli hots it up. The combination works very well and is delicious with cold meat and crusty French bread.

Serves 4
450g/1lb firm ripe tomatoes
½ cucumber
1 onion
1 small hot chilli, seeded and
    chopped and snipped chives,
    to garnish

For the dressing
60ml/4 tbsp olive oil
90ml/6 tbsp thick Greek
    (US strained plain) yogurt
30ml/2 tbsp chopped fresh
    parsley or snipped chives
2.5ml/ ½ tsp white wine vinegar
salt and ground black pepper

1 Peel the tomatoes by first cutting a cross in the base of each tomato. Place in a bowl and cover with boiling water for 30 seconds, or until the skin starts to curl back from the crosses. Drain, plunge into cold water and drain again. Peel, cut the tomatoes into quarters, seed and chop.

2 Chop the cucumber and onion into pieces that are the same size as the tomatoes and put them all in a bowl.

3 To make the dressing, whisk together the oil, yogurt, parsley or chives and vinegar in a bowl and season to taste with salt and pepper. Pour over the salad and toss together. Sprinkle with black pepper and the chopped chilli and chives to garnish.

Cook's Tip
As a light snack, this salad is delicious served with Tomato Toasts. To make the toasts, cut a French loaf diagonally into thin slices. Mix together a crushed garlic clove, a peeled and chopped tomato and 30ml/2 tbsp olive oil. Season with salt and pepper, then spread evenly on the bread and bake at 220°C/425°F/Gas 7 for 10 minutes.

Tomato, Savory & Green Bean Salad

Savory and beans could have been invented for each other. This salad mixes them with ripe tomatoes, and is superb with cold meats.

Serves 4
450g/1lb green beans
1kg/2¼lb ripe tomatoes
3 spring onions (scallions),
    roughly sliced
15ml/1 tbsp pine nuts, toasted
4 fresh savory sprigs

For the dressing
30ml/2 tbsp extra-virgin olive oil
juice of 1 lime
75g/3oz Dolcelatte cheese
1 garlic clove, peeled and crushed
salt and ground black pepper

1 To make the dressing, place all the dressing ingredients in the bowl of a food processor, seasoning with salt and pepper to taste. Process to form a smooth dressing and leave to stand.

2 Top and tail the green beans, then boil in salted water until they are just cooked. Drain the beans and rinse under running cold water until completely cooled. Drain well and transfer to a salad bowl.

3 Slice the tomatoes or, if they are fairly small, quarter them. Add to the green beans, together with the spring onions, and toss together.

4 Pour the dressing onto the salad, toss once more, then sprinkle the pine nuts and savory sprigs over the top and serve.

Cook's Tip
Summer savory has a delicious peppery taste. It is particularly good for enhancing the flavour of beans and peas. The winter variety is sharper and better in dishes such as stuffings.

Cucumber & tomato salad: Energy 156kcal/646kJ; Protein 3g; Carbohydrate 5.8g, of which sugars 5.4g; Fat 13.9g, of which saturates 2.9g; Cholesterol 0mg; Calcium 75mg; Fibre 2.1g; Sodium 32mg
Tomato, savory & bean salad: Energy 211kcal/877kJ; Protein 8.4g; Carbohydrate 11.7g, of which sugars 10.7g; Fat 14.8g, of which saturates 4.9g; Cholesterol 14mg; Calcium 153mg; Fibre 5.2g; Sodium 252mg

Tomato & Bread Salad

This rustic salad, which originally hails from Italy, is a convenient way of using up bread that is a few days old. It is easy to make, but the success of the dish depends on the quality of the tomatoes – they must be ripe and flavourful.

Serves 4
400g/14oz stale white or brown
    bread or rolls
4 large tomatoes
1 large red onion or 6 spring
    onions (scallions)
a few fresh basil leaves, to garnish

For the dressing
60ml/4 tbsp extra-virgin olive oil
30ml/2 tbsp white wine vinegar
salt and ground black pepper

1 Cut the bread or rolls into thick slices. Place in a shallow bowl and soak with cold water. Leave for at least 30 minutes.

2 Cut the tomatoes into chunks and place in a bowl. Finely slice the onion or spring onions and add to the tomatoes.

3 Squeeze as much water out of the bread as possible and add it to the vegetables.

4 To make the dressing, whisk the olive oil with the vinegar, then season with salt and pepper.

5 Pour the dressing over the salad and mix well. Garnish with basil leaves. Allow to stand in a cool place for at least 2 hours.

> **Cook's Tip**
> *Tomatoes left to ripen on the vine will have the best flavour so try to buy "vine-ripened" varieties. Luckily, these are now widely available in supermarkets and more flavourful varieties are now becoming easier to find. However, nothing can beat the taste of home-grown, organic tomatoes. You can use any type of tomato for this dish – halved cherry tomatoes will look attractive or use Italian plum tomatoes for an authentic touch.*

Turkish Tomato Salad

This classic salad is a wonderful combination of textures and flavours. The saltiness of the cheese is perfectly balanced by the refreshing salad vegetables.

Serves 4
1 cos or romaine lettuce heart
1 green (bell) pepper
1 red (bell) pepper
½ cucumber
4 tomatoes
1 red onion
225g/8oz feta cheese, crumbled
black olives, to garnish

For the dressing
45ml/3 tbsp extra-virgin olive oil
45ml/3 tbsp lemon juice
1 garlic clove, crushed
15ml/1 tbsp chopped
    fresh parsley
15ml/1 tbsp chopped fresh mint
salt and ground black pepper

1 Chop the lettuce into bitesize pieces. Quarter the peppers, remove the cores and seeds, then cut the flesh into thin strips. Chop the cucumber and slice or chop the tomatoes. Cut the onion in half, then slice finely.

2 Place the chopped lettuce, peppers, cucumber, tomatoes and onion in a large bowl. Sprinkle the feta over the top and toss together lightly.

3 To make the dressing, blend together the extra-virgin olive oil, lemon juice and garlic in a small bowl or a screw-top jar. Stir in the freshly chopped parsley and mint, and season with salt and pepper to taste.

4 Pour the dressing over the salad, toss lightly with your hands until well coated, then garnish with a few black olives.

> **Variations**
> *• The feta cheese can be substituted with a firm goat's cheese very successfully.*
> *• Try adding croûtons for a contrast in texture – simply cut cubes from day-old bread and fry in olive oil.*

Turkish tomato salad: Energy 276kcal/1146kJ; Protein 11.2g; Carbohydrate 12.1g, of which sugars 11.4g; Fat 20.6g, of which saturates 9.1g; Cholesterol 39mg; Calcium 246mg; Fibre 3.4g; Sodium 827mg
Tomato & bread salad: Energy 354kcal/1496kJ; Protein 9.4g; Carbohydrate 52.9g, of which sugars 6.1g; Fat 13.3g, of which saturates 1.7g; Cholesterol 0mg; Calcium 123mg; Fibre 2.7g; Sodium 530mg

Persian Salad with Tomatoes

This easy-to-make salad is versatile enough to accompany almost any main course dish, but is especially good with chargrilled meat and rice dishes.

Serves 4
4 tomatoes
½ cucumber
1 cos or romaine lettuce heart
1 onion, finely chopped

For the dressing
30ml/2 tbsp olive oil
juice of 1 lemon
1 garlic clove, crushed
salt and ground black pepper

1 Peel the tomatoes by first cutting a cross in the base of each tomato. Place in a bowl and cover with boiling water for 30 seconds, or until the skin starts to curl back from the crosses. Drain, plunge into cold water and drain again. Peel, cut the tomatoes into quarters. Remove the seeds, if you like, and dice the flesh.

2 Cut the cucumber into cubes, removing the skin first if you like. Tear the lettuce into pieces.

3 Place the tomatoes, cucumber, onion and lettuce in a large salad bowl and toss lightly together.

4 To make the dressing, pour the olive oil into a small bowl. Add the lemon juice and garlic and season with salt and pepper. Whisk together well. Alternatively, combine the dressing ingredients in a screw-top jar, close tightly and shake vigorously.

5 Pour the dressing over the salad and toss lightly to mix. Sprinkle with black pepper before serving.

Variation
Use lime juice for this dressing – it will add a deliciously aromatic flavour and it will be slightly sweeter too.

Spicy Tomato & Cucumber Salad

This easy-to-make salad is a particularly good foil to hot curries, with its refreshing ingredients and crunchy texture.

Serves 4–6
2 limes
2.5ml/½ tsp sugar
2 onions, finely chopped

4 firm tomatoes, finely chopped
½ cucumber, finely chopped
1 green chilli, finely chopped
a few fresh coriander (cilantro) leaves, chopped
salt and ground black pepper
a few fresh coriander (cilantro) and mint leaves, to garnish

1 Squeeze the limes into a small bowl and add the sugar with salt and pepper to taste. Leave to rest until the sugar and salt have dissolved. Mix well.

2 Add the onions, tomatoes, cucumber, chilli and the fresh coriander leaves. Chill until ready to serve. Garnish with fresh coriander and mint before serving.

Cook's Tip
Chillies can vary in strength so add a little at a time, according to taste. If you prefer a milder salad, omit the chilli altogether and add extra chopped fresh mint.

Persian salad: Energy 74kcal/307kJ; Protein 1.2g; Carbohydrate 4g, of which sugars 3.9g; Fat 6g, of which saturates 0.9g; Cholesterol 0mg; Calcium 25mg; Fibre 1.5g; Sodium 10mg
Spicy tomato salad: Energy 30kcal/124kJ; Protein 1.2g; Carbohydrate 5.6g, of which sugars 4.8g; Fat 0.4g, of which saturates 0.1g; Cholesterol 0mg; Calcium 33mg; Fibre 1.7g; Sodium 10mg

Simple Pepper Salad

Succulent grilled peppers make a lovely salad.

Serves 4

4 large (bell) peppers, halved and seeded

60ml/4 tbsp olive oil
1 onion, thinly sliced
2 garlic cloves, crushed
4 tomatoes, peeled and chopped
pinch of sugar
5ml/1 tsp lemon juice
salt and ground black pepper

1 Grill (broil) the peppers, skin-side up, until the skins have blistered and charred. Put in a bowl and cover with crumpled kitchen paper. Cool slightly, then remove skins and slice thinly.

2 Heat the oil and fry the onion and garlic until softened. Add the peppers and tomatoes and fry for 10 minutes more. Remove from the heat, stir in the sugar and lemon juice and season. Leave to cool and serve at room temperature.

Roasted Pepper & Tomato Salad

A lovely, colourful dish that is designed to be eaten at room temperature. It is delicious with salamis and savoury flans.

Serves 4

3 red (bell) peppers
6 large plum tomatoes
2.5ml/½ tsp dried red chilli flakes

1 red onion, finely sliced
3 garlic cloves, finely chopped
grated (shredded) rind and juice
    of 1 lemon
45ml/3 tbsp chopped fresh
    flat leaf parsley
30ml/2 tbsp extra-virgin olive oil
salt and ground black pepper
olives and extra chopped flat leaf
    parsley, to garnish

1 Preheat the oven to 220°C/425°F/Gas 7. Place the peppers on a baking sheet and roast, turning occasionally, for 10 minutes or until the skins are almost blackened. Add the tomatoes to the baking sheet and bake for a further 5 minutes.

2 Place the peppers in a strong polythene bag, close the top loosely, trapping in the steam. Set aside, with the tomatoes until cool enough to handle.

3 Carefully remove the skins from the peppers. Remove the core and seeds, then chop the peppers and tomatoes roughly and place in a mixing bowl.

4 Add the chilli flakes, onion, garlic and lemon rind and juice. Sprinkle over the parsley. Mix and transfer to a serving dish.

5 Sprinkle with a little salt and black pepper, drizzle over the olive oil and scatter the olives and extra parsley over the top. Serve at room temperature.

> **Cook's Tip**
> *Roasting or grilling (broiling) the peppers brings out their sweet flavour and makes them meltingly soft. This cooking process also loosens the pepper skins, making them easy to remove.*

Romanian Pepper Salad

This is traditionally made with long sweet peppers, but bell peppers would also work well.

Serves 4

8 long green and/or orange
    peppers, halved and seeded
1 garlic clove, crushed

60ml/4 tbsp wine vinegar
75ml/5 tbsp olive oil
salt and ground black pepper
4 tomatoes, sliced
1 red onion, thinly sliced
fresh coriander (cilantro) sprigs,
    to garnish

1 Grill (broil) the peppers, skin-side up, until the skins have blistered and charred. Transfer to a bowl and cover with crumpled kitchen paper or cling film (plastic wrap).

2 When the peppers are cool enough to handle. slip and peel the skins off and cut each piece in half lengthwise.

3 Mix the garlic and vinegar in a bowl, then whisk in the olive oil. Season to taste.

4 Arrange the peppers, tomatoes and onion on four serving plates and pour over the garlic dressing. If desired, season with more black pepper and serve, garnished with fresh coriander sprigs. The peppers taste good chilled but are best served freshly made at room temperature.

Simple pepper salad: Energy 161kcal/670kJ; Protein 2.1g; Carbohydrate 12.3g, of which sugars 11.6g; Fat 11.8g, of which saturates 1.8g; Cholesterol 0mg; Calcium 21mg; Fibre 3.2g; Sodium 15mg
Roasted pepper & tomato salad: Energy 122kcal/510kJ; Protein 2.5g; Carbohydrate 14.3g, of which sugars 13.5g; Fat 6.5g, of which saturates 1.1g; Cholesterol 0mg; Calcium 24mg; Fibre 3.8g; Sodium 18mg
Romanian pepper salad: Energy 203kcal/841kJ; Protein 2.5g; Carbohydrate 16g, of which sugars 15g; Fat 14.7g, of which saturates 2.2g; Cholesterol 0mg; Calcium 23mg; Fibre 3.9g; Sodium 11mg

Chargrilled Pepper & Pasta Salad

The simple addition of fresh basil and coriander to this pepper and pasta salad give it loads of flavour. A lemon and pesto dressing brings all the flavours together making this an ideal side dish for a summery al fresco meal.

Serves 4
1 large red (bell) pepper
1 large green (bell) pepper
250g/9oz/2¼ cups dried fusilli
   tricolore pasta

1 handful fresh basil leaves,
   roughly torn
1 handful fresh coriander
   (cilantro) leaves, roughly torn
1 garlic clove
salt and ground black pepper

For the dressing
30ml/2 tbsp pesto
juice of ½ lemon
60ml/4 tbsp extra-virgin olive oil

1 Put the peppers under a hot grill (broiler) and grill (broil) for about 10 minutes, turning frequently, until the skins have blistered and charred. Transfer to a bowl, cover with crumpled kitchen paper and set aside until cool.

2 Meanwhile, bring a large pan of salted water to the boil. Add the pasta and cook according to the instructions on the packet.

3 Whisk all the dressing ingredients together in a large mixing bowl. Drain the cooked pasta and add to the bowl of dressing. Toss well to mix and set aside to cool.

4 Rinse the cooled peppers under cold running water. Peel off the skins. Cut the peppers in half, remove the cores and seeds, then pat dry on kitchen paper. Chop and add to the pasta.

5 Stir the basil and parsley into the pasta and toss well to mix, then taste and adjust the seasoning, if necessary.

Cook's Tip
Fusilli tricolore are small, red, white and green pasta spirals.

Spanish Salad with Capers & Olives

Make this refreshing salad in the summer when tomatoes are at their sweetest and full of flavour. Serve with warm ciabatta or walnut bread.

Serves 4
4 tomatoes
½ cucumber
1 bunch spring onions (scallions),
   trimmed and chopped

1 bunch watercress
8 stuffed olives
30ml/2 tbsp drained capers

For the dressing
30ml/2 tbsp red wine vinegar
5ml/1 tsp paprika
2.5ml/½ tsp ground cumin
1 garlic clove, crushed
75ml/5 tbsp extra-virgin olive oil
salt and ground black pepper

1 Using a sharp knife, make a small cross on the top of the tomatoes, then plunge into a bowl of boiling water for 30 seconds. Peel, then finely dice the flesh. Put in a salad bowl.

2 Peel the cucumber, dice finely and add to the tomatoes. Add half the spring onions to the salad bowl and mix lightly. Break the watercress into sprigs. Add to the tomato mixture, with the olives and capers.

3 To make the dressing, mix the wine vinegar, paprika, cumin and garlic in a bowl. Whisk in the oil and add salt and pepper to taste. Pour over the salad and toss lightly. Serve immediately with the remaining spring onions.

Chargrilled pepper salad: Energy 481kcal/2025kJ; Protein 13.2g; Carbohydrate 70.8g, of which sugars 8.5g; Fat 18.1g, of which saturates 3.2g; Cholesterol 4mg; Calcium 99mg; Fibre 4.6g; Sodium 51mg
Spanish salad with capers & olives: Energy 172kcal/712kJ; Protein 2.5g; Carbohydrate 5g, of which sugars 4.3g; Fat 16g, of which saturates 2.4g; Cholesterol 0mg; Calcium 71mg; Fibre 2.2g; Sodium 305mg

Mushroom Salad

This simple refreshing salad is often served as part of a selection of vegetable salads, or crudités. Leaving it to stand before serving brings out the inherent sweetness of the mushrooms.

Serves 4

175g/6oz white mushrooms, trimmed
grated (shredded) rind and juice of 1½ lemons
about 30–45ml/2–3 tbsp crème fraîche or soured cream
salt and white pepper
15ml/1 tbsp chopped fresh chives, to garnish

1 Slice the mushrooms thinly and place in a bowl.

2 Add the lemon rind and juice and the cream, adding a little more cream if needed.

3 Stir gently to mix, then season with salt and pepper.

4 Leave the salad to stand for at least 1 hour to allow the flavours to develop. Stir occasionally.

5 Sprinkle the salad with chopped chives before serving.

Variations
• Add colour and a nutty flavour by sustituting all or half of the white mushrooms with chestnut mushrooms, which are widely available.
• If you prefer, toss the mushrooms in a little vinaigrette – simply make the vinaigrette by whisking 60ml/4 tbsp walnut oil or extra-virgin olive oil into the lemon juice.
• This salad has a freshness and texture that make it the perfect accompaniment to chilli con carne. Use lime, rather than lemon juice, to complement the chillies. Serve the creamy mushrooms on top of shredded iceberg lettuce, with a hunk of warm crusty bread and a hearty bowl of chilli, for the perfect winter supper.

Salad of Fresh Ceps

Mushrooms can make a marvellous salad, especially if you are able to obtain fresh ceps or porcini. Any wild or cultivated mushrooms can be used: remove the stems from shiitake mushrooms.

Serves 4

350g/12oz fresh ceps, thinly sliced
175g/6oz mixed salad leaves, preferably including batavia, young spinach and frisée
50g/2oz/½ cup broken walnut pieces, toasted
50g/2oz piece Parmesan cheese
salt and ground black pepper

For the dressing
2 egg yolks
2.5ml/½ tsp French mustard
75ml/5 tbsp groundnut oil
45ml/3 tbsp walnut oil
30ml/2 tbsp lemon juice
30ml/2 tbsp chopped fresh parsley
pinch of caster (superfine) sugar

1 To make the dressing, place the egg yolks in a screw-top jar with the mustard, groundnut and walnut oils, lemon juice, parsley and sugar. Close the jar tightly and shake well.

2 Place the mushrooms in a large mixing bowl and pour over the dressing. Toss to coat, then set aside for 10–15 minutes to allow the flavours to mingle.

3 Add the salad leaves to the mushrooms and toss lightly. Season with plenty of salt and pepper.

4 Divide the salad among four large plates. Sprinkle each portion with the toasted walnuts and shavings of Parmesan cheese. Serve immediately.

Cook's Tip
The dressing for this salad uses raw egg yolk. Be sure to use only the freshest eggs from a reputable supplier. Expectant mothers, young children and the elderly are advised to avoid raw egg yolks. The dressing can be made without the egg yolks.

Mushroom salad: Energy 22kcal/93kJ; Protein 1.1g; Carbohydrate 0.6g, of which sugars 0.5g; Fat 1.8g, of which saturates 1g; Cholesterol 5mg; Calcium 17mg; Fibre 0.7g; Sodium 7mg
Salad of fresh ceps: Energy 388kcal/1603kJ; Protein 10.1g; Carbohydrate 1.5g, of which sugars 1.3g; Fat 38g, of which saturates 6.8g; Cholesterol 113mg; Calcium 191mg; Fibre 1.8g; Sodium 147mg

Bulgur Wheat Salad

Bursting with summery flavours, this salad has a delicious texture and makes a change from a rice or pasta salad. Bulgur wheat is easy to prepare, too.

Serves 4

225g/8oz/1⅓ cups bulgur wheat
350ml/12fl oz/1½ cups
    vegetable stock
1 cinnamon stick
generous pinch of ground cumin
pinch of cayenne pepper
pinch of ground cloves
5ml/1 tsp salt
10 mangetouts (snow peas),
    topped and tailed

1 red and 1 yellow (bell) pepper,
    roasted, skinned, seeded
    and diced
2 plum tomatoes, peeled, seeded
    and diced
2 shallots, finely sliced
5 black olives, pitted and cut into
    quarters
30ml/2 tbsp each chopped fresh
    basil, mint and parsley
30ml/2 tbsp roughly chopped
    walnuts
30ml/2 tbsp balsamic vinegar
120ml/4fl oz/½ cup extra-virgin
    olive oil
ground black pepper
onion rings, to garnish

1 Place the bulgur wheat in a large bowl. Pour the stock into a pan and bring to the boil with the spices and salt.

2 Cook the stock for 1 minute, then pour, with the cinnamon stick, over the wheat. Leave to stand for 30 minutes.

3 In another bowl, mix together the mangetouts, peppers, tomatoes, shallots, olives, herbs and walnuts. Add the vinegar, olive oil and a little black pepper and stir thoroughly to mix.

4 Strain the bulgur wheat of any liquid and discard the cinnamon stick. Place in a serving bowl, stir in the fresh vegetable mixture and serve, garnished with onion rings.

Cook's Tip
Fresh herbs are essential for this salad. Dried herbs will not make a suitable substitute.

Thai Rice Salad

This is a lovely, soft, fluffy rice dish, perfumed with limes and fresh lemon grass.

Serves 4

2 limes
1 lemon grass stalk
225g/8oz/generous 1 cup brown
    long grain rice
15ml/1 tbsp olive oil
1 onion, chopped
2.5cm/1in piece fresh root ginger,
    peeled and finely chopped

7.5ml/1½ tsp coriander seeds
7.5ml/1½ tsp cumin seeds
750ml/1¼ pints/3 cups
    vegetable stock
60ml/4 tbsp chopped fresh
    coriander (cilantro)
spring onion (scallion) finely sliced,
    and toasted coconut strips,
    to garnish
lime wedges, to serve

1 Pare the limes using a canelle knife (zester) or a fine grater, taking care to avoid cutting the bitter pith. Set aside. Finely chop the lower portion of the lemon grass stalk and set aside.

2 Rinse the rice in plenty of cold water until the water runs clear. Turn into a sieve (strainer) and drain thoroughly.

3 Heat the olive oil in a pan. Add the onion, ginger, spices, lemon grass and lime rind and cook gently over a low heat, stirring occasionally, for about 3 minutes until the onion is soft.

4 Add the drained rice and cook. stirring constantly, for 1 minute, then pour in the stock and bring to the boil.

5 Reduce the heat to very low and cover the pan with a tight-fitting lid. Cook gently for 30 minutes, then check the rice. If it is still crunchy, re-cover and leave for 3–5 minutes more. Remove the pan from the heat when done.

6 Stir in the fresh coriander, fluff up the grains, cover the pan again and leave for about 10 minutes.

7 Transfer to a serving dish or individual bowls, garnish with spring onion and toasted coconut, and serve with lime wedges.

Bulgur wheat salad: Energy 429kcal/1782kJ; Protein 7.7g; Carbohydrate 52.1g, of which sugars 8.5g; Fat 21.7g, of which saturates 3g; Cholesterol 0mg; Calcium 70mg; Fibre 3g; Sodium 507mg
Thai rice salad: Energy 125kcal/523kJ; Protein 2.6g; Carbohydrate 20.9g, of which sugars 1.4g; Fat 4.1g, of which saturates 0.6g; Cholesterol 0mg; Calcium 38mg; Fibre 1.3g; Sodium 7mg

Tabbouleh

This is a wonderfully refreshing, tangy salad of soaked bulgur wheat and masses of fresh mint, parsley and spring onions.

Serves 4–6

250g/9oz/1½ cups bulgur wheat
600ml/1 pint/2½ cups water
1 large bunch spring onions
    (scallions), thinly sliced
1 cucumber, finely chopped
    or diced
3 tomatoes, chopped
1.5–2.5ml/¼–½ tsp
    ground cumin
1 large bunch fresh parsley,
    chopped
1 large bunch fresh mint, chopped
juice of 2 lemons, or to taste
60ml/4 tbsp extra-virgin olive oil
salt
cos or romaine lettuce,
    to serve
olives and lemon wedges,
    to garnish

1 Place the bulgur wheat in a bowl, pour over the water and leave to soak for 20 minutes.

2 Line a colander with a clean dish towel. Turn the soaked bulgur wheat into the centre, let it drain, then gather up the sides of the dish towel and squeeze out any remaining liquid. Transfer the bulgur wheat to a large bowl.

3 Add the spring onions to the bulgur wheat, then mix and squeeze together with your hands to combine.

4 Add the cucumber, tomatoes, cumin, parsley and mint and mix well, then pour in the lemon juice and oil. Add salt to taste and toss to combine.

5 Heap the tabbouleh onto a bed of lettuce. Garnish with olives and lemon wedges.

Variations
• Use couscous soaked in boiling water in place of the bulgur wheat.
• Use chopped fresh coriander (cilantro) instead of parsley.
• Try serving the salad with natural (plain) yogurt.

Couscous Salad

Couscous has become an extremely popular salad ingredient, and there are many variations on the classic theme. This salad comes from Morocco.

Serves 4

275g/10oz/1⅔ cups couscous
550ml/18fl oz/2½ cups boiling
    vegetable stock
16–20 pitted black olives, halved
2 small courgettes (zucchini), cut
    into matchstick strips
25g/1oz/¼ cup flaked
    almonds, toasted
60ml/4 tbsp olive oil
15ml/1 tbsp lemon juice
15ml/1 tbsp chopped
    fresh coriander (cilantro)
15ml/1 tbsp chopped fresh
    parsley
good pinch of ground cumin
good pinch of cayenne pepper
salt
sprigs of coriander (cilantro),
    to garnish

1 Place the couscous in a bowl and pour over the boiling stock. Stir with a fork, then set aside for 10 minutes for the stock to be absorbed. Fluff up with a fork.

2 Add the olives, courgettes and almonds to the couscous and mix in gently.

3 Whisk the olive oil, lemon juice, coriander, parsley, cumin, cayenne and a pinch of salt in a bowl. Pour the dressing over the salad and toss to mix. Transfer to a serving dish and garnish with coriander sprigs.

Cook's Tip
This salad benefits from being made several hours ahead.

Variations
• You can substitute ½ cucumber for the courgettes (zucchini) and pistachios for the almonds.
• For extra heat, add a pinch of chilli powder to the dressing.

Tabbouleh: Energy 232kcal/965kJ; Protein 5.2g; Carbohydrate 34.6g, of which sugars 2.7g; Fat 8.4g, of which saturates 1.1g; Cholesterol 0mg; Calcium 51mg; Fibre 1.4g; Sodium 12mg
Couscous salad: Energy 324kcal/1344kJ; Protein 7.1g; Carbohydrate 37.4g, of which sugars 1.8g; Fat 17g, of which saturates 2.1g; Cholesterol 0mg; Calcium 80mg; Fibre 2.1g; Sodium 287mg

Cracked Wheat Salad with Oranges & Almonds

The citrus flavours of lemon and orange really come through in this tasty salad, which can be made several hours before serving.

Serves 4

150g/5oz/scant 1 cup
  bulgur wheat
600ml/1 pint/2½ cups water
1 small green (bell) pepper,
  seeded and diced
¼ cucumber, diced
15g/½oz/½ cup chopped
  fresh mint
60ml/4 tbsp flaked almonds,
  toasted
grated (shredded) rind and juice
  of 1 lemon
2 seedless oranges
salt and ground black pepper
fresh mint sprigs, to garnish

1 Place the bulgur wheat in a bowl, pour over the water and leave to soak for 20 minutes.

2 Line a colander with a clean dish towel. Turn the soaked bulgur wheat into the centre, let it drain, then gather up the sides of the dish towel and squeeze out any remaining liquid. Transfer the bulgur wheat to a large bowl.

3 Add the green pepper, diced cucumber, mint, toasted almonds and grated (shredded) lemon rind. Pour in the lemon juice and toss thoroughly to mix.

4 Cut the skin and pith from the oranges, then, working over a bowl to catch the juice, cut between the membranes to release the segments. Add the segments and the juice to the bulgur mixture, then season to taste with salt and pepper and toss lightly. Garnish with the mint sprigs and serve.

> **Cook's Tip**
> Bulgur wheat is also known as cracked wheat because the grains are cracked after hulling and steaming and before drying.

Lemony Bulgur Wheat Salad

A variation on *tabbouleh*, this salad is delicious as an accompaniment to grilled meats or fish, or on its own as a light snack.

Serves 4

2 tomatoes, peeled and chopped
225g/8oz/1½ cups bulgur wheat
4 spring onions (scallions),
  finely chopped
75ml/5 tbsp chopped fresh basil
75ml/5 tbsp chopped fresh
  parsley
15ml/1 tbsp chopped fresh
  coriander (cilantro)
juice of 1 lemon
75ml/5 tbsp olive oil
salt and ground black pepper
fresh basil sprigs, to garnish

1 Make a slash in the skin of each tomato, then put them all in a heatproof bowl and pour over boiling water. Leave for 30 seconds, then plunge the tomatoes into cold water. Peel and seed, then roughly chop the flesh. Set aside.

2 Place the bulgur wheat in a bowl, pour on enough boiling water to cover and leave to soak for 20 minutes.

3 Line a colander with a clean dish towel. Turn the soaked bulgur wheat into the centre, let it drain, then gather up the sides of the dish towel and squeeze out any remaining liquid. Turn the bulgur wheat into a large bowl.

4 Add the spring onions, mint, parsley, coriander and tomatoes. Mix well, then pour over the lemon juice and olive oil. Season generously with salt and pepper, then toss so that all the ingredients are combined.

5 Chill in the refrigerator for a couple of hours before serving, garnished with mint.

> **Variation**
> Add some pitted, halved black olives to the salad just before serving for extra tangy flavour.

Cracked wheat salad: Energy 254kcal/1060kJ; Protein 7.8g; Carbohydrate 39g, of which sugars 9.8g; Fat 7.9g, of which saturates 0.6g; Cholesterol 0mg; Calcium 96mg; Fibre 3g; Sodium 10mg
Bulgur wheat salad: Energy 194kcal/811kJ; Protein 4.3g; Carbohydrate 31.2g, of which sugars 2.3g; Fat 6.5g, of which saturates 0.9g; Cholesterol 0mg; Calcium 56mg; Fibre 1.6g; Sodium 12mg

Tanzanian Vegetable Rice

This light, fluffy dish of steamed rice flavoured with colourful vegetables makes a versatile accompaniment.

Serves 4–6
350g/12oz/2 cups basmati rice
45ml/3 tbsp vegetable oil

1 onion, chopped
750ml/1¼ pints/3 cups vegetable
   stock or water
2 garlic cloves, crushed
115g/4oz/1 cup sweetcorn
½ fresh red or green (bell)
   pepper, chopped
1 large carrot, grated

1 Rinse the rice in a sieve (strainer) under cold water, then leave to drain for about 15 minutes.

2 Heat the oil in a large pan, add the onion and fry for a few minutes over medium heat until just softened.

3 Add the rice and stir-fry for about 10 minutes, taking care to stir continuously so that the rice does not stick to the bottom of the pan.

4 Add the stock or water and the garlic and stir well. Bring to the boil and cook over high heat for 5 minutes, then reduce the heat, cover with a tight-fitting lid and leave the rice to cook for 20 minutes.

5 Scatter the corn over the rice, then spread the pepper on top and lastly sprinkle over the grated carrot.

6 Cover tightly and continue to steam over low heat until the rice is cooked. Gently fork through the rice to fluff up and serve immediately.

Variation
Vary the vegetables according to what you have to hand. Sliced courgettes (zucchini) or small broccoli florets would work well, while frozen peas make an easy, colourful addition. Defrost them before adding to the rice.

Bulgur Wheat & Cherry Tomato Salad

This appetizing salad is ideal served with fresh crusty bread and home-made chutney or pickle.

Serves 6
350g/12oz/2 cups bulgur wheat
225g/8oz frozen broad
   (fava) beans
115g/4oz/1 cup frozen petits
   pois (baby peas)
225g/8oz cherry tomatoes, halved
1 sweet onion, chopped

1 red (bell) pepper, seeded
   and diced
50g/2oz mangetouts
   (snow peas), chopped
50g/2oz watercress
45ml/3 tbsp chopped fresh
   herbs, such as parsley, basil
   and thyme

For the dressing
75ml/5 tbsp olive oil
15ml/1 tbsp white wine vinegar
5ml/1 tsp mustard powder
salt and ground black pepper

1 Put the bulgur wheat into a large bowl. Add enough cold water to come 2.5cm/1in above the level of the wheat. Leave to soak for approximately 30 minutes.

2 Turn the soaked bulgur wheat into a sieve (strainer) lined with a clean dish towel. Drain the wheat well and use the dish towel to squeeze out any excess water.

3 Cook the broad beans and petits pois in a pan of boiling water for about 3 minutes, until tender. Drain thoroughly and mix with the prepared bulgur wheat in a bowl.

4 Add the cherry tomatoes, onion, pepper, mangetouts and watercress to the bulgur wheat mixture and mix. Combine all the ingredients for the dressing, season and stir well.

5 Add the herbs to the salad, season and add enough dressing to taste. Toss the ingredients together.

6 Serve immediately or cover and chill in the refrigerator before serving.

Tanzanian rice: Energy 449kcal/1877kJ; Protein 8.1g; Carbohydrate 83g, of which sugars 7.7g; Fat 9.3g, of which saturates 1.1g; Cholesterol 0mg; Calcium 30mg; Fibre 1.8g; Sodium 85mg
Bulgur wheat & cherry tomato: Energy 302kcal/1261kJ; Protein 9.8g; Carbohydrate 42.8g, of which sugars 4.9g; Fat 10.8g, of which saturates 1.5g; Cholesterol 0mg; Calcium 84mg; Fibre 5g; Sodium 17mg

Nutty Red Bean & Pasta Salad

An unusual combination of nuts, pasta shells and colourful vegetables, this substantial salad makes an interesting starter. The creamy spiced dressing gives the dish a hot tangy bite.

Serves 4
1 onion, cut into 12 rings
115g/4oz/³⁄₄ cup canned red
  kidney beans, drained
1 courgette (zucchini), sliced
1 yellow courgette, sliced
50g/2oz pasta shells, cooked
50g/2oz/¹⁄₂ cup cashew nuts
25g/1oz/¹⁄₄ cup peanuts

lime wedges and fresh coriander
  (cilantro) sprigs, to garnish

For the dressing
120ml/4 fl oz/¹⁄₂ cup fromage
  frais or crème fraîche
30ml/2 tbsp natural (plain) yogurt
1 green chilli, chopped
15ml/1 tbsp chopped fresh
  coriander (cilantro)
2.5ml/¹⁄₂ tsp salt
2.5ml/¹⁄₂ tsp crushed black
  peppercorns
2.5ml/¹⁄₂ tsp crushed dried red
  chillies
15ml/1 tbsp lemon juice

1 Arrange the onion rings, red kidney beans, green and yellow courgette slices and pasta shells in a salad dish, ready for serving. Sprinkle the cashew nuts and peanuts over the top.

2 To make the dressing, place the fromage frais in a separate bowl with the yogurt, green chilli, coriander and salt. Beat well together with a fork.

3 Sprinkle the crushed black peppercorns, red chillies and lemon juice over the dressing.

4 Garnish the salad with the lime wedges and coriander sprigs and serve the dressing separately or poured over the salad.

> **Cook's Tips**
> • For wholesome finger food at a party, try serving the salad stuffed into mini pitta breads. Omit the beans, if you like.
> • Toast the nuts in a dry frying pan (skillet) for extra crunch.

Chickpea & Egg Salad

Topped with hard-boiled eggs, this substantial salad is good with smoked fish.

Serves 4–6
2 x 400g/14oz cans chickpeas, or
  300g/11oz/2 cups cooked
  chickpeas
6 spring onions (scallions),
  chopped
2 tomatoes, diced
1 small red onion, finely chopped

12 black olives, pitted and halved
15ml/1 tbsp capers, drained
30ml/2 tbsp finely chopped fresh
  parsley or mint leaves
4 hard-boiled (hard-cooked) eggs,
  cut into quarters, to garnish

For the dressing
75ml/5 tbsp olive oil
45ml/3 tbsp wine vinegar
salt and ground black pepper

1 Rinse the chickpeas under cold running water. Drain and place in a serving bowl. Add the spring onions, tomatoes, red onion, olives, capers and parsley or mint.

2 To make the dressing, whisk all the ingredients together in a small bowl. Add to the salad, toss and serve with the eggs.

> **Variation**
> Other types of canned cooked beans may be substituted in this salad, such as cannellini or borlotti beans.

Nutty pasta salad: Energy 236kcal/980kJ; Protein 9.2g; Carbohydrate 15.1g, of which sugars 6.1g; Fat 15.8g, of which saturates 4.3g; Cholesterol 3mg; Calcium 102mg; Fibre 3.5g; Sodium 167mg

Chickpea salad: Energy 305kcal/1275kJ; Protein 14.4g; Carbohydrate 23.5g, of which sugars 2.4g; Fat 17.8g, of which saturates 2.9g; Cholesterol 127mg; Calcium 90mg; Fibre 6.3g; Sodium 531mg

White Bean & Celery Salad

This simple bean salad is a delicious alternative to the potato salad that seems to appear on every salad menu. If you do not have time to soak and cook dried beans, use canned ones.

Serves 4
450g/1lb dried white beans (haricot, cannellini, navy or butter (lima) beans) or 3 x 400g/14oz cans white beans

1 litre/1¾ pints/4 cups vegetable stock
3 celery sticks, cut into 1cm/½in strips
120ml/4fl oz/½ cup French dressing
45ml/3 tbsp chopped fresh parsley
salt and ground black pepper

1 If you are using dried beans, cover them with plenty of cold water and soak for at least 4 hours. Discard the soaking water, then place the beans in a heavy pan. Cover with water.

2 Bring to the boil and simmer without a lid for 1½ hours, or until the skins are broken. Cooked beans will squash readily between a thumb and forefinger. Drain the beans. If using canned beans, drain and rinse.

3 Place the cooked beans in a large pan. Add the vegetable stock and celery, bring to the boil, cover and simmer for 15 minutes. Drain thoroughly. Moisten the beans with the French dressing and leave to cool.

4 Add the chopped parsley and mix. Season to taste with salt and pepper, transfer to a salad bowl and serve.

Cook's Tip
To make a French dressing, whisk 90ml/6tbsp extra-virgin olive oil with about 15ml/1 tbsp each white wine vinegar and balsamic vinegar, 5ml/1 tsp French mustard, a little sugar and salt and pepper to taste. Vary the vinegar quantity to taste.

Broad Bean & Feta Salad

This recipe is loosely based on a typical medley of fresh-tasting Greek salad ingredients – broad beans, tomatoes and feta cheese. It is lovely as a starter, served warm or cold and accompanied by pitta bread.

Serves 4–6
900g/2lb broad (fava) beans, shelled, or 350g/12oz shelled frozen beans

60ml/4 tbsp olive oil
175g/6oz plum tomatoes, halved, or quartered if large
4 garlic cloves, crushed
115g/4oz/1 cup firm feta cheese, cut into chunks
45ml/3 tbsp chopped fresh dill
12 black olives
salt and ground black pepper
chopped fresh dill, to garnish

1 Cook the fresh or frozen broad beans in boiling, salted water until just tender. Drain and set aside.

2 Meanwhile, heat the oil in a heavy-based frying pan (skillet) and add the tomatoes and garlic. Cook until the tomatoes are beginning to colour.

3 Add the feta cheese to the pan and toss the ingredients together for 1 minute. Mix with the drained beans, chopped dill, and black olives. Season with salt and pepper to taste and serve garnished with chopped dill.

White bean & celery salad: Energy 496kcal/2082kJ; Protein 25.1g; Carbohydrate 49.9g, of which sugars 3.1g; Fat 16.5g, of which saturates 3.2g; Cholesterol 0mg; Calcium 125mg; Fibre 17.9g; Sodium 313mg
Broad bean & feta salad: Energy 175kcal/727kJ; Protein 8.3g; Carbohydrate 8.8g, of which sugars 2.2g; Fat 12g, of which saturates 3.8g; Cholesterol 13mg; Calcium 121mg; Fibre 4.7g; Sodium 342mg

Peppery Bean Salad

This pretty salad uses canned beans for speed and convenience. Hot pepper sauce gives a bit of a kick.

Serves 4–6
425g/15oz can red kidney beans
425g/15oz can black-eyed beans
425g/15oz can chickpeas
¼ red (bell) pepper
¼ green (bell) pepper
6 radishes

15ml/1 tbsp chopped spring
  onion (scallion), plus extra sliced
  to garnish

For the dressing
5ml/1 tsp ground cumin
15ml/1 tbsp tomato ketchup
30ml/2 tbsp olive oil
15ml/1 tbsp white wine vinegar
1 garlic clove, crushed
2.5ml/½ tsp hot pepper sauce

1 Drain the red kidney beans, black-eyed beans and chickpeas and rinse under cold running water. Shake off the excess water and turn them into a large bowl.

2 Core, seed and chop the red and green peppers. Trim the radishes and slice thinly. Add the peppers, radishes and spring onion to the beans.

3 Mix together the cumin, ketchup, oil, vinegar and garlic in a small bowl. Add a little salt and hot pepper sauce to taste and stir again thoroughly.

4 Pour the dressing over the salad and toss to mix well. Chill the salad for at least 1 hour before serving, garnished with the sliced spring onion.

Variations
• *To make a tasty tuna salad, make up the dressing without the cumin. Drain a 200g/7oz can tuna, flake the flesh and stir into the bean salad. Add some lightly cooked, halved green beans, hard-boiled (hard-cooked) egg and tomato quarters.*
• *For extra flavour and colour, stir in a handful of pitted black olives and a handful of chopped fresh parsley.*

Broad Bean Salad

The Moroccan technique of marrying broad beans with preserved lemons creates a flavourful side salad.

Serves 4
2kg/4½lb broad (fava) beans
  in the pod
60–75ml/4–5 tbsp olive oil

juice of ½ lemon
2 garlic cloves, chopped
5ml/1 tsp ground cumin
10ml/2 tsp paprika
small bunch of fresh coriander
  (cilantro)
1 preserved lemon, chopped
handful of black olives, to garnish
salt and ground black pepper

1 Bring a large pan of salted water to the boil. Meanwhile, pod the broad beans. Put the shelled beans in the pan and boil for about 2 minutes.

2 Drain and refresh the beans under cold running water. Drain well. Slip off and discard the thick outer skin to reveal the smooth, bright green beans underneath.

3 Put the beans in a heavy pan and add the olive oil, lemon juice, garlic, cumin and paprika. Cook the beans gently over a low heat for about 10 minutes, then season to taste with salt and pepper and leave to cool in the pan until warm.

4 Transfer the warm beans to a serving bowl, scraping all the juices from the pan. Finely chop the fresh coriander and add to the beans with the preserved lemon. Toss together, then garnish with the black olives and serve immediately.

Cook's Tip
To make preserved lemons, scrub and quarter lemons almost through to the base, then rub the cut sides with salt. Pack tightly into a large sterilized jar. Half fill the jar with more salt, adding some bay leaves, peppercorns and cinnamon, if you like. Cover completely with lemon juice. Cover with a lid and store for 2 weeks, shaking the jar daily. Add a little olive oil to seal and use within 1–6 months, washing off the salt before use.

Butter Bean & Red Onion Salad

This quick and easy salad can be assembled ahead of time, making it ideal for entertaining. It is particularly useful for eating al fresco and is delicious as an accompaniment to meat cooked on a barbecue.

Serves 4
2 x 400g/14oz cans butter
   (lima) beans
4 plum tomatoes,
   roughly chopped
1 red onion, finely sliced
45ml/3 tbsp herb-infused olive oil
salt and ground black pepper

1 Drain the beans and rinse under cold running water. Drain well and mix with the tomatoes and onion in a large bowl.

2 Season with salt and pepper to taste and stir in the herb-infused olive oil. Transfer to a serving dish.

3 Cover the bowl with clear film (plastic wrap) and chill for 20 minutes before serving.

Variation
To make a wholesome version of the Italian salad Panzanella, tear half a loaf of ciabatta into bitesize pieces and stir into the salad. Leave to stand for 20 minutes before serving.

Brown Bean Salad

Brown beans, sometimes called *ful medames*, are available from health-food shops and Middle-Eastern grocery stores. Dried broad beans or black or red kidney beans make a good substitute.

Serves 6
350g/12oz/1½ cups dried
   brown beans
3 fresh thyme sprigs
2 bay leaves
1 onion, halved

4 garlic cloves, crushed
7.5ml/1½ tsp crushed
   cumin seeds
3 spring onions (scallions),
   finely chopped
90ml/6 tbsp chopped
   fresh parsley
20ml/4 tsp lemon juice
90ml/6 tbsp olive oil
3 hard-boiled (hard-cooked) eggs,
   roughly chopped
1 pickled cucumber,
   roughly chopped
salt and ground black pepper

1 Put the beans in a bowl with plenty of cold water and leave to soak overnight. Drain, transfer to a pan and cover with fresh water. Bring to the boil and boil rapidly for 10 minutes.

2 Reduce the heat and add the thyme, bay leaves and onion. Simmer very gently for about 1 hour, until tender. Drain and discard the herbs and onion.

3 Place the beans in a large bowl. Mix together the garlic, cumin seeds, spring onions, parsley, lemon juice and oil in a small bowl, and add a little salt and pepper. Pour over the beans and toss the ingredients lightly together.

4 Gently stir in the chopped hard-boiled eggs and pickled cucumber. Transfer the bean salad to a serving dish and serve immediately.

Variation
To ring the changes, try using crumbled feta cheese or goat's cheese instead of the hard-boiled (hard-cooked) egg.

Butter bean & red onion salad: Energy 251kcal/1055kJ; Protein 12.7g; Carbohydrate 30.3g, of which sugars 6.2g; Fat 9.6g, of which saturates 1.5g; Cholesterol 0mg; Calcium 41mg; Fibre 10.4g; Sodium 850mg
Brown bean salad: Energy 300kcal/1258kJ; Protein 16.6g; Carbohydrate 27.1g, of which sugars 2.5g; Fat 14.8g, of which saturates 2.5g; Cholesterol 95mg; Calcium 99mg; Fibre 9.9g; Sodium 50mg

Chicory, Fruit & Nut Salad

The mildly bitter taste of the attractive white chicory leaves combines wonderfully well with sweet fruit, and is especially delicious when complemented by a creamy curry sauce.

Serves 4

45ml/3 tbsp mayonnaise
15ml/1 tbsp Greek (US strained
   plain) yogurt
15ml/1 tbsp mild curry paste
90ml/6 tbsp single (light) cream
1/2 iceberg lettuce
2 chicory (Belgian endive) heads
50g/2oz/1/2 cup cashew nuts
50g/2oz/1 1/4 cups flaked coconut
2 red apples
75g/3oz/1/3 cup currants

1 Mix the mayonnaise, yogurt, curry paste and single cream in a small bowl. Cover and chill until required.

2 Tear the lettuce into pieces and put into a mixing bowl.

3 Cut the root end off each head of chicory, separate the leaves and add them to the lettuce. Preheat the grill (broiler).

4 Grill (broil) the cashew nuts for 2 minutes, until golden. Transfer to a bowl and set aside. Spread out the coconut on a baking sheet. Grill for 1 minute, until golden.

5 Quarter the apples and cut out the cores. Slice the apples and add them to the lettuce with the toasted coconut and cashew nuts and the currants.

6 Spoon the dressing over the salad, toss lightly and serve.

Cook's Tips
• Watch the coconut flakes and cashew nuts with great care when they are under the grill, as they brown very fast.
• This lightly spiced salad is excellent served as a side dish to perk up plainly grilled chicken or lamb chops.

Apple & Celeriac Salad

Celeriac, despite its coarse appearance, has a sweet and subtle flavour. Traditionally par-boiled in lemony water, in this salad it is served raw, allowing its unique taste and texture to come through.

Serves 3–4

675g/1 1/2lb celeriac, peeled
10–15ml/2–3 tsp lemon juice
5ml/1 tsp walnut oil (optional)
1 apple
45ml/3 tbsp mayonnaise
10ml/2 tsp Dijon mustard
15ml/1 tbsp chopped
   fresh parsley
salt and ground black pepper

1 Using a food processor or coarse cheese grater, shred the celeriac. Alternatively, cut it into very thin julienne strips. See the cook's tip below.

2 Place the prepared celeriac in a bowl and sprinkle with the lemon juice and the walnut oil, if using. Stir well to mix.

3 Peel the apple if you like. Cut the apple into quarters and remove the core. Slice the apple quarters thinly crossways and toss together with the celeriac.

4 Whisk together the mayonnaise, mustard and parsley, seasoning with salt and pepper to taste.

5 Add the dressing to the celeriac mixture and stir well. Chill the salad for several hours until ready to serve.

Cook's Tip
Celeriac browns very quickly. If you are grating or slicing it by hand, you will need to add lemon juice frequently to prevent discoloration. One way to do this is to grate the celeriac over a bowl of lemony water. If you are hand cutting julienne strips, have a bowl of lemony water beside you and drop the strips in as you go. Drain the celeriac and squeeze out excess water when you have finished.

Chicory, fruit & nut salad: Energy 319kcal/1327kJ; Protein 5.1g; Carbohydrate 20.9g, of which sugars 18.2g; Fat 24.5g, of which saturates 9.3g; Cholesterol 21mg; Calcium 84mg; Fibre 3.4g; Sodium 120mg
Apple & celeriac salad: Energy 99kcal/410kJ; Protein 1.2g; Carbohydrate 3.5g, of which sugars 3.4g; Fat 9.1g, of which saturates 1.3g; Cholesterol 8mg; Calcium 73mg; Fibre 2.1g; Sodium 226mg

Yogurt & Grape Salad

Raitas cool the effect of hot curries. Cucumber and mint raita is most common, but why not try this variation?

Serves 4

350ml/12fl oz/1½ cups natural (plain) yogurt
75g/3oz seedless grapes, washed and dried
50g/2oz shelled walnuts
2 firm bananas
5ml/1 tsp sugar
5ml/1 tsp freshly ground cumin seeds
salt
2.5ml/½ tsp freshly roasted cumin seeds, chilli powder or paprika, to garnish

1 Place the yogurt in a chilled bowl and add the grapes and walnuts. Slice the bananas directly into the bowl and fold in gently before the bananas turn brown.

2 Add the sugar, salt and ground cumin, and gently mix together. Chill, and just before serving, sprinkle over the cumin seeds, chilli powder or paprika.

Variation
Try using roughly chopped pecan nuts or roasted hazelnuts instead of walnuts, and adding chopped apple with the grapes.

Apple, Beetroot & Red Leaf Salad

Bitter salad leaves are complemented by sweet-flavoured apples and juicy beetroot in this side salad.

Serves 4

50g/2oz/⅓ cup whole unblanched almonds
2 red apples, cored and diced
juice of ½ lemon
115g/4oz/4 cups red salad leaves, such as lollo rosso, oakleaf and radicchio
200g/7oz pre-cooked beetroot (beet) in natural juice, sliced

For the dressing
30ml/2 tbsp olive oil
15ml/1 tbsp walnut oil
15ml/1 tbsp red or white wine vinegar
salt and ground black pepper

1 Toast the almonds in a dry frying pan for 2–3 minutes until golden brown, tossing frequently to prevent them burning

2 Meanwhile, make the dressing. Put the olive and walnut oils, vinegar and salt and pepper in a bowl or screw-top jar. Stir or shake thoroughly to combine.

3 Toss the apples in lemon juice to prevent them browning, then place in a large bowl and add the salad leaves, beetroot and almonds.

4 Pour over the dressing and toss gently to disperse the ingredients evenly.

Cook's Tips
• Try to use fresh, raw beetroot (beet) if it is available. Cooking fresh beetroot is surprisingly easy – the important thing is not to puncture the skin before cooking, otherwise the bright red juice will leak out. To prepare fresh beetroot, trim off most of the leafy stalks, then wash and cook the unpeeled roots in boiling water for 1–2 hours, depending on size.
• Red fruits and vegetables have high levels of vitamins C and E and beta carotene.

Yogurt & grape salad: Energy 189kcal/792kJ; Protein 6.9g; Carbohydrate 20.5g, of which sugars 19.5g; Fat 9.6g, of which saturates 1.2g; Cholesterol 1mg; Calcium 184mg; Fibre 1g; Sodium 74mg
Apple & beetroot salad: Energy 216kcal/895kJ; Protein 4.1g; Carbohydrate 9.5g, of which sugars 8.8g; Fat 18.2g, of which saturates 1.9g; Cholesterol 0mg; Calcium 54mg; Fibre 2.7g; Sodium 58mg

Carrot, Raisin & Apricot Coleslaw

A tasty variation on classic coleslaw, this colourful salad combines cabbage, carrots and two kinds of dried fruit in a yogurt dressing.

Serves 6
350g/12oz/3 cups white cabbage
225g/8oz/1½ cups carrots
1 red onion, finely sliced
3 celery sticks, sliced
175g/6oz/generous 1 cup raisins

75g/3oz/½ cup dried
  apricots, chopped

For the dressing
120ml/4fl oz/½ cup mayonnaise
90ml/6 tbsp natural (plain) yogurt
30ml/2 tbsp chopped fresh
  mixed herbs
salt and ground black pepper

1 Finely shred the cabbage and coarsely grate (shred) the carrots. Place both in a large mixing bowl.

2 Add the onion, celery, raisins and apricots to the cabbage and carrots and mix well.

3 In a small bowl, mix together the mayonnaise and yogurt, then stir in the chopped fresh mixed herbs. Season with salt and pepper to taste.

4 Add the mayonnaise dressing to the coleslaw ingredients and toss together to mix. Cover and chill before serving.

Fruit & Nut Coleslaw

A delicious and nutritious mixture of crunchy vegetables, fruit and nuts, tossed together in a mayonnaise dressing.

Serves 6
225g/8oz white cabbage
1 large carrot
175g/6oz/¾ cup ready-to-eat
  dried apricots

50g/2oz/ ½ cup walnuts
50g/2oz/ ½ cup hazelnuts
115g/4oz/ ⅔ cup raisins
30ml/2 tbsp chopped
  fresh parsley
105ml/7 tbsp mayonnaise
75ml/5 tbsp natural (plain) yogurt
salt and ground black pepper
fresh chives, to garnish

1 Finely shred the cabbage and coarsely grate (shred) the carrot. Place both in a large mixing bowl.

2 Roughly chop the dried apricots, walnuts and hazelnuts. Stir them into the cabbage and carrot mixture with the raisins and chopped parsley.

3 In a separate bowl, mix together the mayonnaise and yogurt and season to taste with salt and pepper.

4 Add the mayonnaise mixture to the cabbage mixture and toss together to mix. Cover and set aside in a cool place for at least 30 minutes before serving, to allow the flavours to mingle. Garnish with a few fresh chives and serve.

Variations
• For a salad that is lower in fat, use low-fat natural (plain) yogurt and reduced-calorie mayonnaise.
• Instead of walnuts and hazelnuts, use flaked almonds and chopped pistachios.
• Omit the dried apricots and add a cored and chopped unpeeled eating apple.
• Substitute other dried fruit or a mixture for the apricots – try nectarines, peaches or prunes.

Carrot, raisin & apricot coleslaw: Energy 263kcal/1099kJ; Protein 3g; Carbohydrate 29.4g, of which sugars 28.8g; Fat 15.7g, of which saturates 2.4g; Cholesterol 15mg; Calcium 92mg; Fibre 3.2g; Sodium 143mg
Fruit & nut coleslaw: Energy 309kcal/1285kJ; Protein 4.3g; Carbohydrate 19.1g, of which sugars 18.8g; Fat 24.5g, of which saturates 2.9g; Cholesterol 13mg; Calcium 72mg; Fibre 2.5g; Sodium 103mg

Orange & Chicory Salad

Chicory and oranges are both winter ingredients, so this salad is perfect as a light accompaniment to hearty winter meat dishes. The fresh flavours also go well with seafood dishes.

Serves 6
2 chicory (Belgian endive) heads
2 oranges
30ml/2 tbsp extra-virgin olive oil
25g/1oz/2 tbsp walnut halves,
    roughly chopped
salt and ground black pepper

1 Trim off the bottom of each chicory head and separate the leaves. Arrange on a serving platter.

2 Place one of the oranges on a chopping board and slice off the top and bottom to expose the flesh. Place the orange upright and, using a small sharp knife, slice down between the skin and the flesh. Do this all the way around until the orange is completely free of peel and pith. Repeat with the remaining orange, reserving any juice.

3 Holding one orange over a bowl to catch the juices, cut between the membrane to release the segments. Repeat with the second orange.

4 Arrange the orange segments on the platter with the chicory.

5 Whisk the oil with any juice from the oranges, and season with salt and pepper to taste. Sprinkle the walnuts over the salad, drizzle over the dressing and serve immediately.

Cook's Tip
Blood oranges look especially attractive served in this dish. Mandarins give a subtly different flavour that some prefer.

Variation
Use young spinach leaves or rocket (arugula) instead of chicory.

Carrot & Orange Salad

This classic fruit and vegetable combination makes a wonderful, fresh-tasting salad. A great side dish for the winter months, it is particularly good with hot or cold poultry dishes.

Serves 4
450g/1lb carrots
2 large oranges
15ml/1 tbsp olive oil
30ml/2 tbsp lemon juice
pinch of sugar (optional)
30ml/2 tbsp chopped pistachio
    nuts or toasted pine nuts
salt and ground black pepper

1 Peel the carrots and grate (shred) them into a large serving bowl.

2 Cut a slice off the top and bottom of one orange. Place the orange upright on a board and cut off the skin, taking care to remove all the bitter white pith. Repeat with the second orange, reserving any juice. Working over a bowl to catch the juices, cut between the membranes to release the segments.

3 Whisk together the olive oil, lemon juice and reserved orange juice in a bowl. Season with a little salt and pepper to taste, and add sugar, if you like.

4 Toss the orange segments together with the carrots and pour the dressing over. Scatter the salad with the pistachio nuts or pine nuts before serving.

Orange & chicory salad: Energy 81kcal/335kJ; Protein 1.2g; Carbohydrate 4.6g, of which sugars 3.9g; Fat 6.8g, of which saturates 0.8g; Cholesterol 0mg; Calcium 31mg; Fibre 1.2g; Sodium 3mg
Carrot & orange salad: Energy 137kcal/571kJ; Protein 2.9g; Carbohydrate 15.9g, of which sugars 15.1g; Fat 7.3g, of which saturates 1.1g; Cholesterol 0mg; Calcium 72mg; Fibre 4.4g; Sodium 72mg

Fennel, Orange & Rocket Salad

This light and refreshing salad is ideal to serve with spicy or rich foods. Zesty orange blends perfectly with the delicate flavour of fennel and the peppery rocket.

Serves 4
2 oranges, such as Jaffa, Shamouti
   or blood oranges
1 fennel bulb

115g/4oz rocket (arugula) leaves
50g/2oz/⅓ cup black olives

For the dressing
30ml/2 tbsp extra-virgin olive oil
15ml/1 tbsp balsamic vinegar
1 small garlic clove, crushed
salt and ground black pepper

1 Using a vegetable peeler, pare off strips of rind from the oranges, leaving the pith behind, then cut the pared rind into thin julienne strips. Blanch the strips in boiling water for a few minutes. Drain and set aside.

2 Cut a slice off the top and bottom of one orange. Place the orange upright on a board and cut off the skin, taking care to remove all the bitter white pith. Repeat with the second orange, reserving any juice. Slice the oranges into thin rounds.

3 Trim the fennel bulb, then cut in half lengthwise and slice across the bulb as thinly as possible, preferably in a food processor fitted with a slicing disc or using a mandolin.

4 Combine the slices of orange and fennel in a serving bowl and toss with the rocket leaves.

5 To make the dressing, mix together the oil, vinegar and garlic and season with salt and pepper to taste. Pour over the salad, toss together well and leave to stand for a few minutes. Sprinkle with the black olives and julienne strips of orange.

Variation
For a twist in flavour, substitute minneolas for the oranges.

Orange & Red Onion Salad

Cumin and mint give this refreshing, quick-to-prepare salad a very Middle-Eastern flavour. Small, seedless oranges are most suitable, if available.

Serves 6
6 oranges
2 red onions
15ml/1 tbsp cumin seeds
5ml/1 tsp coarsely ground
   black pepper
15ml/1 tbsp chopped fresh mint
90ml/6 tbsp olive oil
salt
fresh mint sprigs and black
   olives, to serve

1 Slice the oranges thinly, catching any juices. Holding each orange slice in turn over a bowl, cut round with scissors to remove the peel and pith. Reserve the juice.

2 Slice the onions thinly and separate into rings.

3 Arrange the orange and onion slices in layers in a shallow dish, sprinkling each layer with cumin seeds, black pepper, chopped mint, olive oil and salt to taste. Pour over the reserved orange juice.

4 Leave the salad to marinate in a cool place for 2 hours.

5 Scatter over the mint sprigs and black olives, and serve.

Fennel, orange & rocket salad: Energy 113kcal/469kJ; Protein 2.5g; Carbohydrate 9.9g, of which sugars 9.8g; Fat 7.3g, of which saturates 1g; Cholesterol 0mg; Calcium 116mg; Fibre 3.9g; Sodium 332mg
Orange & red onion salad: Energy 199kcal/825kJ; Protein 1.6g; Carbohydrate 11.5g, of which sugars 11.3g; Fat 16.6g, of which saturates 2.4g; Cholesterol 0mg; Calcium 68mg; Fibre 2.3g; Sodium 7mg

Asparagus & Orange Salad

This is a slightly unusual combination of ingredients with a simple dressing based on good-quality olive oil.

Serves 4

225g/8oz asparagus, trimmed and cut into 5cm/2in lengths
2 large oranges
2 well-flavoured tomatoes, cut into eighths
50g/2oz cos lettuce leaves
30ml/2 tbsp extra-virgin olive oil
2.5ml/½ tsp sherry vinegar
salt and ground black pepper

1 Cook the asparagus in boiling, salted water for 3–4 minutes, until just tender. The cooking time may vary according to the size of the asparagus stems. Drain and refresh under cold water, then leave on one side to cool.

2 Grate (shred) the rind from half one orange and reserve.

3 Cut a slice off the top and bottom of one orange to reveal the flesh. Place the orange upright on a board and, using a small sharp knife, cut off the skin, taking care to remove all the bitter white pith. Repeat with the second orange, reserving any juice.

4 Holding one orange over a bowl to catch the juices, cut between the membrane to release the segments. Repeat with the second orange. Reserve the juices.

5 Put the asparagus, orange segments, tomatoes and lettuce in a salad bowl.

6 Mix together the oil and vinegar, and add 15ml/1 tbsp of the reserved orange juice and 5ml/1 tsp of the grated rind. Season with salt and pepper to taste. Just before serving, pour the dressing over the salad and mix gently to coat the ingredients.

Cook's Tip
Do not overcook the asparagus; it should still be quite firm.

Black & Orange Salad

This dramatically colourful salad is ideal for serving with plainly grilled or barbecued meat and fish.

Serves 4

3 oranges
115g/4oz/1 cup pitted black olives
15ml/1 tbsp chopped fresh coriander (cilantro)
15ml/1 tbsp chopped fresh parsley

For the dressing
30ml/2 tbsp olive oil
15ml/1 tbsp lemon juice
2.5ml/½ tsp paprika
2.5ml/½ tsp ground cumin

1 Cut a slice off the top and bottom of one orange to reveal the flesh. Place the orange upright on a board and, using a small sharp knife, cut off the skin, taking care to remove all the bitter white pith. Repeat with the remaining oranges, then cut between the membranes to release the segments.

2 Place the orange segments in a salad bowl and add the black olives, coriander and parsley.

3 To make the dressing, blend together the olive oil, lemon juice, paprika and cumin.

4 Pour the dressing over the salad and toss gently. Chill for about 30 minutes and serve.

Variation
The strong flavours and vivid colours of this salad work brilliantly with couscous. Adapt the recipe by chopping the orange segments and olives quite finely (using a mandolin makes this a quick and easy job). Mix the finely chopped olives and oranges with the herbs and dressing into a bowl of cooked couscous while it is still warm. Either chill the salad or serve it immediately. It's delicious cold or warm – and perfect for a picnic with cold chicken or smoked ham.

Asparagus & orange salad: Energy 92kcal/384kJ; Protein 2.6g; Carbohydrate 7.2g, of which sugars 7.1g; Fat 6.1g, of which saturates 0.9g; Cholesterol 0mg; Calcium 46mg; Fibre 2.4g; Sodium 8mg
Black & orange salad: Energy 129kcal/537kJ; Protein 1.8g; Carbohydrate 11.1g, of which sugars 10.6g; Fat 9g, of which saturates 1.3g; Cholesterol 0mg; Calcium 79mg; Fibre 3g; Sodium 654mg

Orange & Water Chestnut Salad

Crisp water chestnuts combine with oranges to make a colourful and clean-tasting salad.

Serves 4
2 oranges
1 red onion, thinly sliced into rings
1 400g/14oz can drained water chestnuts, peeled and cut into strips
2 radicchio heads, cored, or 1 red-leaf lettuce, leaves separated
45ml/3 tbsp chopped fresh parsley
45ml/3 tbsp chopped fresh basil
15ml/1 tbsp white wine vinegar
50ml/2fl oz/¼ cup walnut oil
salt and ground black pepper
1 fresh basil sprig, to garnish

1 Cut a slice off the top and bottom of one orange to reveal the flesh. Place the orange upright on a board and, using a small sharp knife, cut off the skin, taking care to remove all the bitter white pith. Repeat with the remaining orange.

2 Holding one peeled orange over a bowl, cut between the membranes to release the segments. Repeat with the remaining orange. Discard the membranes.

3 Put the onion in a colander and sprinkle with 5ml/1 tsp salt. Allow to drain for 15 minutes.

4 Put the oranges in a large bowl, add the water chestnuts and toss to mix.

5 Rinse the onion to remove excess salt and pat dry on kitchen paper. Toss with the water chestnuts and oranges.

6 Spread out the radicchio or red-leaf lettuce leaves in a large, shallow bowl or on a serving platter. Arrange the water chestnut, orange and onion mixture on top. Sprinkle with the chopped parsley and basil.

7 Put the vinegar, oil and salt and pepper to taste in a screw-top jar and shake well to combine. Pour the dressing over the salad and serve immediately, garnished with a sprig of basil.

Plantain & Green Banana Salad

The plantains and bananas are cooked in their skins to keep their soft texture. They then absorb all the flavour of the dressing.

Serves 4
2 firm yellow plantains
3 green bananas
1 garlic clove, crushed
1 red onion
15–30ml/1–2 tbsp chopped fresh coriander (cilantro)
45ml/3 tbsp sunflower oil
25ml/1½ tbsp malt vinegar
salt and ground black pepper

1 Slit the plantains and bananas lengthwise along their natural ridges, then cut in half and place in a large pan.

2 Cover the plantains and bananas with water, add a little salt and bring to the boil. Boil gently for 20 minutes, until tender, then remove from the water. When they are cool enough to handle, peel and cut into medium-size slices.

3 Put the plantain and banana slices into a bowl and add the garlic, turning them with a wooden spoon to distribute the garlic evenly.

4 Halve the onion and slice thinly. Add to the bowl with the coriander, oil, vinegar and seasoning. Toss together to mix, then transfer to a serving bowl.

Orange & water chestnut: Energy 110kcal/458kJ; Protein 1.5g; Carbohydrate 6.9g, of which sugars 6.6g; Fat 8.8g, of which saturates 0.8g; Cholesterol 0mg; Calcium 59mg; Fibre 2g; Sodium 20mg
Plantain & green banana salad: Energy 242kcal/1019kJ; Protein 2.2g; Carbohydrate 40.9g, of which sugars 21g; Fat 8.9g, of which saturates 1.2g; Cholesterol 0mg; Calcium 35mg; Fibre 2.5g; Sodium 8mg

Date, Orange & Carrot Salad

Rojak

Take exotic fresh dates and marry them with everyday ingredients, such as carrots and oranges, to create this deliciously different salad. It is excellent served with chargrilled lamb steaks or skewered lamb.

Serves 4
3 carrots
3 oranges
2 Little Gem (Bibb) lettuce, leaves separated
115g/4oz fresh dates, stoned (pitted) and cut into eighths
25g/1oz/¼ cup toasted whole almonds, chopped
salt and ground black pepper

1 Grate (shred) the carrots. Using a sharp knife, cut the peel and pith away from two of the oranges. Cut between the membranes to release the segments. Reserve any juice.

2 Line a serving dish or four individual plates with lettuce. Pile the grated carrots on top and arrange the peeled orange segments next to the carrot, pouring any extra juice over them Season with salt and ground black pepper

3 Pile the dates on top of the carrots, then sprinkle with the chopped, toasted almonds.

4 Squeeze the juice from the remaining orange and sprinkle over the salad. Chill the salad for an hour before serving.

In Indonesia and Malaysia, there are many versions of this salad, but all feature a selection of fruit and vegetables in a tangy sauce.

half a pomelo, separated into segments, membrane removed
a handful of beansprouts, washed and drained
fresh mint leaves, to garnish

Serves 4–6
1 jicama (sweet turnip), peeled and finely sliced
1 small cucumber, partially peeled and finely sliced
1 green mango, peeled and finely sliced
1 star fruit (carambola), sliced
4 slices fresh pineapple, cored

For the sauce
225g/8oz/2 cups roasted peanuts
4 garlic cloves, chopped
2–4 red chillies, seeded and chopped
10ml/2 tsp shrimp paste, dry-roasted in a pan over a high heat
15ml/1 tbsp tamarind paste
30ml/2 tbsp palm sugar (jaggery)
salt

1 First make the sauce. Using a mortar and pestle or food processor, grind the peanuts with the garlic and chillies to a coarse paste. Beat in the roasted shrimp paste, tamarind paste and sugar.

2 Add enough water to make a thick, pouring sauce, and stir until the sugar has dissolved. Add salt to taste.

3 Arrange all the sliced fruit and vegetables on a plate, with the beansprouts scattered over the top.

4 Drizzle the sauce over the salad, garnish with mint leaves and serve immediately as an accompaniment to grilled (broiled) meats and spicy dishes.

Cook's Tip
Shrimp paste (terasi) can be bought from Asian food stores. It should always be cooked before use.

Date, orange & carrot salad: Energy 147kcal/620kJ; Protein 3.8g; Carbohydrate 25g, of which sugars 24.3g; Fat 4.3g, of which saturates 0.5g; Cholesterol 0mg; Calcium 103mg; Fibre 5.3g; Sodium 34mg
Rojak: Energy 330Kcal/1381kJ; Protein 12.9g; Carbohydrate 28g, of which sugars 25.1g; Fat 19.3g, of which saturates 3.4g; Cholesterol 13mg; Calcium 114mg; Fibre 6.3g; Sodium 416mg

Vietnamese Fruit Salad

Simple and attractive, this arranged salad makes a delightful accompaniment to lightly spiced finger food.

Serves 4–6

1 crunchy lettuce, leaves separated
½ cucumber, peeled and thinly sliced
1–2 carrots, finely sliced
200g/7oz/scant 1 cup beansprouts
1–2 unripe star fruit, finely sliced
1–2 green bananas, finely sliced
1 firm papaya, halved, seeded, peeled and finely sliced
1 bunch each fresh mint and basil, stalks removed
juice of 1 lime

1 Arrange the all the salad ingredients attractively on a plate, with the lettuce leaves on one side to use as wrappers.

2 Squeeze the lime juice over the fruits, particularly the bananas to help them retain their colour, and place the salad in the middle of the table.

Green Mango Salad

This exotic salad is delicious served with stir-fried prawns or seared beef. Green mangoes have dark green skins and light green flesh.

Serves 4

450g/1lb green mangoes
rind and juice of 2 limes
30ml/2 tbsp sugar
30ml/2 tbsp nuoc mam
2 green Thai chillies, seeded and finely sliced
1 small bunch fresh coriander (cilantro), stalks removed, finely chopped
salt

1 Peel, halve and stone (pit) the mango, then slice into thin strips.

2 In a bowl, mix together the lime juice and rind, sugar and nuoc mam. Add the mango strips with the chillies and coriander. Add salt to taste and leave to stand for 20 minutes to allow the flavours to mingle before serving.

Fruity Gado-Gado

This Indonesian salad is distinguished by the peanut and coconut sauce served with it, and is perfect with a variety of spicy dishes.

Serves 6

½ cucumber
2 pears (not too ripe) or 175g/6oz wedge of yam bean
1–2 eating apples
juice of ½ lemon
mixed salad leaves
6 small tomatoes, cut in wedges
3 slices fresh pineapple, cored and cut in wedges
3 eggs, hard-boiled and shelled

175g/6oz egg noodles, cooked, cooled and chopped
deep-fried onions, to garnish

For the peanut sauce

2–4 fresh red chillies, seeded and ground, or 15ml/1 tbsp chilli sambal
300ml/½ pint/1¼ cups coconut milk
350g/12oz/1¼ cups crunchy peanut butter
15ml/1 tbsp dark soy sauce or dark brown sugar
5ml/1 tsp tamarind pulp, soaked in 45ml/3 tbsp warm water
coarsely crushed peanuts
salt

1 To make the peanut sauce, put the ground chillies or chilli sambal in a pan. Pour in the coconut milk, then stir in the peanut butter. Heat gently, stirring, until well blended.

2 Simmer gently until the sauce thickens, then stir in the soy sauce or sugar. Strain in the tamarind liquid, add salt to taste and stir well. Spoon into a bowl and sprinkle with a few coarsely crushed peanuts.

3 To make the salad, core the cucumber and peel the pears or yam bean. Cut them into matchsticks. Finely shred the apples and sprinkle them with the lemon juice.

4 Spread a bed of lettuce leaves on a flat platter or a section of banana leaf, then pile the prepared fruit and vegetables on top.

5 Add the sliced or quartered hard-boiled eggs, the chopped noodles and the deep-fried onions. Serve at once, with the sauce.

Vietnamese fruit salad: Energy 108kcal/455kJ; Protein 4g; Carbohydrate 21g, of which sugars 12g; Fat 1g, of which saturates 0g; Cholesterol 0mg; Calcium 110mg; Fibre 42g; Sodium 0.02mg
Green mango salad: Energy 92kcal/391kJ; Protein 1g; Carbohydrate 22g, of which sugars 15g; Fat 0g, of which saturates 0g; Cholesterol 0mg; Calcium 32mg; Fibre 33g; Sodium 0.5mg
Fruity gado-gado: Energy 490Kcal/2043kJ; Protein 18.9g; Carbohydrate 28.5g, of which sugars 21g; Fat 34.3g, of which saturates 8.6g; Cholesterol 116mg; Calcium 80mg; Fibre 6.2g; Sodium 493mg

Mixed Salad with Lettuce Wraps

Traditionally, an Asian-style table salad is served to accompany spring rolls and pork or shrimp balls, where pieces of the salad might be wrapped around a meaty morsel. The vegetables and fruit in this dish are usually folded into little packets using lettuce leaves or rice wrappers, and then dipped in a sauce, or added bit by bit to bowls of rice or noodles.

Serves 4–6

1 crunchy lettuce, leaves separated
1/2 cucumber, peeled and thinly sliced
2 carrots, finely sliced
200g/7oz/1 cup beansprouts
2 unripe star fruit, finely sliced
2 green bananas, finely sliced
1 firm papaya, cut in half, seeds removed, peeled and finely sliced
leaves from 1 bunch fresh mint and leaves from 1 bunch fresh basil
juice of 1 lime
dipping sauce, to serve

1 Wash all the cut fruit and vegetables, leaves and herbs under cold running water and drain them thoroughly.

2 Arrange the salad ingredients attractively on a large plate, with the lettuce leaves placed on one side so that they can be used as wrappers.

3 Squeeze the lime juice over the sliced fruits, particularly the bananas, to help them retain their colour, and place the salad in the middle of the table.

4 Serve the salad with a dipping sauce of your choice.

Cook's Tip
As this salad is meant to be eaten in the hand, supply guests with some napkins, plus finger bowls filled with warm water. Add some lime and lemon slices to the water so that everyone can freshen up afterwards.

Cucumber Jewel Salad

With its clean taste and bright, jewel-like colours, this salad makes a perfect accompaniment to a variety of spicy dishes and curries. Pomegranate seeds, though not traditional, make a beautiful garnish.

Serves 8

1 small cucumber
1 onion, thinly sliced
1 small, ripe pineapple or 425g/15oz can pineapple rings
1 green (bell) pepper, seeded and thinly sliced
3 firm tomatoes, chopped
30ml/2 tbsp sugar
45–60ml/3–4 tbsp white wine vinegar
120ml/4fl oz/1/2 cup water
salt
seeds of 1–2 pomegranates, to garnish

1 Halve the cucumber lengthways, remove the seeds, slice and spread on a plate with the onion. Sprinkle with salt. After about 10 minutes, rinse off the salt thoroughly and pat dry.

2 If using a fresh pineapple, peel and core it, removing all the eyes, then cut it into bitesize pieces. If using canned pineapple, drain the rings and cut them into small wedges. Place the pineapple in a bowl with the cucumber, onion, green pepper and tomatoes.

3 Heat the sugar, vinegar and measured water in a pan, stirring until the sugar has dissolved. Remove the pan from the heat and leave to cool. When cold, add a little salt to taste and pour over the fruit and vegetables. Cover and chill until required. Serve in small bowls, garnished with pomegranate seeds.

Variation
To make this Indonesian-style, salt a salad cucumber as described in the recipe. Make half the dressing and pour it over the cucumber. Add a few chopped spring onions (scallions). Cover and chill. Serve scattered with toasted sesame seeds.

Mixed salad lettuce wraps: Energy 107kcal/453kJ; Protein 3.1g; Carbohydrate 23g, of which sugars 20.6g; Fat 0.9g, of which saturates 0.2g; Cholesterol 0mg; Calcium 72mg; Fibre 3.8g; Sodium 14mg
Cucumber jewel salad: Energy 53kcal/224kJ; Protein 0.9g; Carbohydrate 12.3g, of which sugars 12.1g; Fat 0.3g, of which saturates 0.1g; Cholesterol 0mg; Calcium 20mg; Fibre 1.5g; Sodium 6mg

Radish, Mango & Apple Salad

Clean, crisp tastes and mellow flavours make this salad a good choice at any time, although it is at its best with fresh garden radishes in early summer.

Serves 4
10–15 radishes
1 eating apple
2 celery stalks, thinly sliced
1 small ripe mango
fresh dill sprigs, to garnish

For the dressing
120ml/4fl oz/ ½ cup
   crème fraîche
10ml/2 tsp creamed horseradish
15ml/1 tbsp chopped fresh dill
salt and ground black pepper

1 To make the dressing, mix the crème fraîche with the creamed horseradish and dill in a small bowl. Season with a little salt and pepper.

2 Top and tail the radishes, then slice them thinly. Place in a large bowl. Cut the apple into quarters, remove the cores from each wedge, then slice the flesh thinly and add it to the bowl with the thinly sliced celery.

3 Cut through the mango lengthwise either side of the stone (pit). Leaving the skin on each section, cross hatch the flesh, then bend it back so that the cubes stand proud of the skin. Slice them off with a small knife and add them to the bowl.

4 Pour the dressing over the vegetables and fruit and stir gently to coat. When ready to serve, spoon the salad into a salad bowl and garnish with the dill.

Cook's Tip
Radishes are members of the mustard family and may be red or white, round or elongated. They vary considerably in their strength of flavour; small, slender French radishes are especially mild and sweet. Whatever type you are buying, look for small, firm, brightly coloured specimens, with no sign of limpness.

Pear & Pecan Nut Salad

Toasted pecan nuts have a special affinity with crisp white pears. Their robust flavours combine well with a rich cheese and chive dressing to make this a salad to remember.

Serves 4
75g/3oz/1½ cup shelled pecan
   nuts, roughly chopped
3 crisp pears
1 escarole or round
   (butterhead) lettuce
1 radicchio
175g/6oz young spinach,
   stems removed
30ml/2 tbsp blue cheese and
   chive dressing
salt and ground black pepper
crusty bread, to serve

1 Toast the shelled pecan nuts under a medium grill (broiler) to bring out their flavour.

2 Cut the pears into even slices, leaving the skins intact but discarding the cores.

3 Separate the leaves on the lettuce and radicchio, then place in a large bowl with the spinach. Add the pear slices and toasted pecans.

4 Pour over the blue cheese dressing and toss well. Distribute among four large serving plates and season with salt and pepper. Serve the salad with warm crusty bread.

Cook's Tips
• *To make blue cheese and chive dip, add 50ml/2fl oz/ ¼ cup soured cream and 50g/2oz crumbled blue cheese to 75ml/3fl oz/⅓ cup mayonnaise. Stir in a few drops of white wine vinegar, 15ml/1 tbsp snipped fresh chives and ground black pepper to taste. Beat well to combine.*
• *The pecan nuts will burn quickly under the grill, so keep a constant watch over them and remove them as soon as they change colour.*

Radish, mango & apple salad: Energy 77kcal/324kJ; Protein 1.4g; Carbohydrate 7.6g, of which sugars 7g; Fat 4.9g, of which saturates 3.1g; Cholesterol 0mg; Calcium 44mg; Fibre 1.4g; Sodium 46mg
Pear & pecan nut salad: Energy 233kcal/965kJ; Protein 4.2g; Carbohydrate 15.3g, of which sugars 14.9g; Fat 17.6g, of which saturates 1.2g; Cholesterol 3mg; Calcium 129mg; Fibre 5.1g; Sodium 151mg

Avocado, Orange & Almond Salad

A wonderful combination of creamy avocado with fresh-tasting oranges and tomatoes, this salad is bursting with authentic Spanish flavours. Serve with chunks of rustic bread, flavoured with sun-dried tomato, for a substantial side dish.

Serves 4
2–3 oranges
2 ripe tomatoes
2 small avocados
60ml/4 tbsp extra-virgin olive oil
30ml/2 tbsp lemon juice
15ml/1 tbsp chopped parsley
small onion rings
25g/1oz/¼ cup split,
    toasted almonds
10–12 black olives
salt and ground black pepper

1 Peel the oranges and slice them into thick rounds. Make a cut in the top of the tomatoes, then plunge them into boiling water for 30 seconds. Lift out with a slotted spoon and refresh in cold water. Peel away the skins, cut the tomatoes into quarters, remove the seeds and chop roughly.

2 Cut the avocados in half, remove the stones (pits) and carefully peel away the skin. Cut into chunks.

3 Mix together the olive oil, lemon juice and parsley. Season with salt and pepper, then toss the avocado and tomatoes in half of the dressing.

4 Arrange the sliced oranges on a plate and scatter with the onion rings. Drizzle with the remaining dressing. Spoon the avocados, tomatoes, almonds and olives on top of the oranges and serve immediately.

> **Cook's Tip**
> *Spanish onions are perfect for this dish as they are sweet and mild, and pleasant to eat raw, but they are very large. Slice them and use just the small central rings for salads, keeping the large outer rings for frying.*

Avocado & Pink Grapefruit Salad

A refreshing and attractive citrus and avocado salad, ideal with grilled oily fish.

Serves 8
mixed red and green lettuce
    or other salad leaves
2 sweet pink grapefruits
1 large or 2 small avocados,
    peeled, stoned (pitted)
    and cubed

For the dressing
90ml/6 tbsp extra-virgin olive oil
30ml/2 tbsp red wine vinegar
1 garlic clove, crushed
5ml/1 tsp Dijon mustard
salt and ground black pepper

For the caramelized peel
4 oranges
50g/2oz/¼ cup caster
    (superfine) sugar
60ml/4 tbsp cold water

1 To make the caramelized peel, using a vegetable peeler, carefully remove the rind from the oranges in thin strips and reserve the fruit. Scrape away the white pith from the underside of the rind with a small, sharp knife, and cut the rind into fine shreds.

2 Put the sugar and water in a small pan and heat gently until the sugar has dissolved. Add the shreds of orange rind, increase the heat and boil steadily for 5 minutes, or until the rind is tender. Using two forks, remove the orange rind from the syrup and spread it out on a wire rack to dry. Reserve the cooking syrup to add to the dressing.

3 Wash and dry the lettuce or other salad leaves and tear or chop them into bitesize pieces. Using a sharp knife, remove the pith from the oranges and the pith and peel from the grapefruit. Hold the citrus fruits over a bowl and cut out each segment leaving the membrane behind. Squeeze the remaining juice from the membrane into the bowl.

4 Put all the dressing ingredients into a screw-top jar and shake well. Add the reserved syrup and adjust the seasoning to taste. Arrange the salad ingredients on plates with the cubed avocado. Spoon over the dressing and sprinkle with the caramelized peel. Serve immediately.

Avocado & pink grapefruit salad: Energy 151kcal/624kJ; Protein 1.1g; Carbohydrate 5.6g, of which sugars 5.1g; Fat 13.9g, of which saturates 2.4g; Cholesterol 0mg; Calcium 24mg; Fibre 1.9g; Sodium 12mg
Avocado, orange & almond salad: Energy 286kcal/1183kJ; Protein 3.5g; Carbohydrate 7.3g, of which sugars 6.4g; Fat 27.1g, of which saturates 4.4g; Cholesterol 0mg; Calcium 70mg; Fibre 4.4g; Sodium 575mg

Pumpkin Salad

Red wine vinegar brings out the sweetness of the pumpkin. No salad leaves are used, just plenty of fresh parsley. A great dish for a cold buffet.

Serves 4

200ml/7fl oz/scant 1 cup olive oil
60ml/4 tbsp red wine vinegar
675g/1½lb pumpkin, peeled and
    cut into 4cm/1½ in pieces
40g/1½oz/¾ cup fresh flat leaf
    parsley leaves, chopped
salt and ground black pepper
fresh flat leaf parsley sprigs, to
    garnish (optional)

1 large red onion, peeled and very
    thinly sliced

1 Mix the onion, olive oil and vinegar in a large bowl. Season with salt and pepper, then stir well to combine.

2 Put the pumpkin pieces in a large pan of cold salted water. Bring to the boil, then lower the heat and simmer gently for 15–20 minutes. Drain.

3 Immediately add the drained pumpkin to the bowl containing the dressing and toss lightly with your hands. Leave to cool. Stir in the chopped parsley, cover with clear film (plastic wrap) and chill until needed.

4 Allow the salad to come back to room temperature before serving. Garnish with fresh parsley sprigs, if you like.

Squash à la Grecque

This recipe, usually made with mushrooms, also works well with patty pan squash. Make sure that you cook the baby squash until they are quite tender, so they absorb the delicious flavours of the marinade.

Serves 4

175g/6oz patty pan squash
250ml/8fl oz/1 cup white wine
juice of 2 lemons

1 fresh thyme sprig
1 bay leaf
small bunch fresh chervil,
    roughly chopped
1.5ml/¼ tsp crushed
    coriander seeds
1.5ml/¼ tsp crushed
    black peppercorns
75ml/5 tbsp olive oil
150ml/¼ pint/⅔ cup water
bay leaves, to garnish

1 Blanch the patty pan squash in boiling water for 3 minutes, then refresh them in cold water.

2 Place the wine, lemon juice, thyme sprig, bay leaf, chervil, coriander seeds, black peppercorns and oil in a pan. Add the water, cover and simmer for 10 minutes.

3 Add the patty pan squash and cook for 10 minutes until they are tender. Using a slotted spoon, transfer the cooked squash to a serving dish.

4 Reduce the liquid in the pan by boiling vigorously for 10 minutes, then strain and pour over the squash. Leave to cool to allow the flavours to be absorbed. Serve the squash cold, garnished with bay leaves.

Cook's Tip
Patty pan squashes are a type of summer squash, and have thin skins and tender flesh. They are treated rather like courgettes (zucchini), which are also a member of the squash family. Winter squashes, such as butternut squash, have much harder skins and are not suitable for this recipe.

Pumpkin salad: Energy 404kcal/1663kJ; Protein 1.7g; Carbohydrate 5.2g, of which sugars 4g; Fat 42g, of which saturates 6.1g; Cholesterol 0mg; Calcium 73mg; Fibre 2.4g; Sodium 4mg
Squash à la Grecque: Energy 171kcal/704kJ; Protein 0.4g; Carbohydrate 1.4g, of which sugars 1.1g; Fat 13.8g, of which saturates 2g; Cholesterol 0mg; Calcium 18mg; Fibre 0.5g; Sodium 3mg

Aubergine, Lemon & Caper Salad

This cooked vegetable relish is delicious served as an accompaniment to cold meats or with pasta.

Serves 4
1 large aubergine (eggplant), about 675g/1 ½lb
60ml/4 tbsp olive oil
grated (shredded) rind and juice of 1 lemon
30ml/2 tbsp capers, rinsed
12 pitted green olives
30ml/2 tbsp chopped fresh flat leaf parsley
salt and ground black pepper

1 Cut the aubergine into 2.5cm/1in cubes. Heat the olive oil in a large frying pan and cook the aubergine cubes over a medium heat for about 10 minutes, tossing regularly, until golden and soft. You may need to do this in two batches. Drain on kitchen paper and sprinkle with a little salt.

2 Place the aubergine cubes in a large serving bowl. Toss with the lemon rind and juice, capers, olives and chopped parsley. Season well with salt and pepper. Serve at room temperature.

Cook's Tip
This will taste even better when made the day before. It will store, covered, in the refrigerator for up to 4 days.

Spiced Aubergine Salad

The delicate flavours of aubergine, tomatoes and cucumber are lightly spiced with cumin and coriander in this fresh-tasting salad. Topped with refreshing yogurt, this salad is the ideal accompaniment to grilled fish or a rice dish.

Serves 4
2 small aubergines (eggplants), sliced
75ml/5 tbsp extra-virgin olive oil
50ml/2fl oz/¼ cup red wine vinegar
2 garlic cloves, crushed
15ml/1 tbsp lemon juice
2.5ml/½ tsp ground cumin
2.5ml/½ tsp ground coriander
½ cucumber, thinly sliced
2 well-flavoured tomatoes, thinly sliced
30ml/2 tbsp natural (plain) yogurt
salt and ground black pepper
chopped fresh flat leaf parsley, to garnish

1 Preheat the grill (broiler). Lightly brush the aubergine slices with olive oil and cook under a high heat, turning once, until golden and tender.

2 When the aubergine slices are done, transfer them to a chopping board and cut them into quarters.

3 Mix together the remaining oil, the vinegar, garlic, lemon juice, cumin and coriander. Season with salt and pepper to taste and mix thoroughly.

4 Add the warm aubergines, stir well and chill for at least 2 hours. Add the cucumber and tomatoes. Transfer to a serving dish and spoon the yogurt on top. Sprinkle with parsley and serve immediately.

Cook's Tip
Cook the aubergines on a ridged cast-iron griddle pan, if you prefer. Heat the griddle pan and cook the aubergine slices for 6-8 minutes on each side, brushing with more oil as necessary.

Aubergine, lemon & caper salad: Energy 141kcal/585kJ; Protein 2g; Carbohydrate 4.1g, of which sugars 3.7g; Fat 13.2g, of which saturates 2g; Cholesterol 0mg; Calcium 50mg; Fibre 4.4g; Sodium 289mg
Spiced aubergine salad: Energy 161kcal/669kJ; Protein 2.3g; Carbohydrate 5.8g, of which sugars 5.5g; Fat 14.6g, of which saturates 2.2g; Cholesterol 0mg; Calcium 37mg; Fibre 3.7g; Sodium 15mg

Grilled Leek & Fennel Salad with Spicy Tomato Dressing

This is an excellent salad for the early autumn, when leeks are at their best and tomatoes are full of flavour.

Serves 6

675g/1½lb leeks
2 large fennel bulbs
120ml/4fl oz/½ cup olive oil
2 shallots, chopped
150ml/¼ pint/⅔ cup dry white wine or white vermouth
5ml/1 tsp fennel seeds, crushed
6 fresh thyme sprigs
2–3 bay leaves
pinch of dried red chilli flakes
350g/12oz tomatoes, peeled, seeded and diced
5ml/1 tsp sun-dried tomato paste (optional)
good pinch of sugar (optional)
75g/3oz/¾ cup small black olives
salt and ground black pepper

1 Cook the leeks in boiling salted water for 4–5 minutes. Using a slotted spoon, place them in a colander to drain and cool. Then cut into 7.5cm/3in lengths. Reserve the cooking water.

2 Trim and slice the fennel. Keep the tops for a garnish. Cook the fennel in the reserved water for about 5 minutes, drain, then toss with 30ml/2 tbsp of olive oil. Season to taste.

3 On a ridged cast iron griddle, grill (broil) the vegetables until tinged deep brown, then place them in a large shallow dish.

4 Heat the remaining oil, the shallots, white wine or vermouth, crushed fennel seeds, thyme, bay leaves and chilli flakes in a large pan and bring to the boil over a medium heat. Lower the heat and simmer for 10 minutes.

5 Add the diced tomoes and cook briskly until the consistency of the dressing has thickened. Add the tomato paste and adjust the seasoning, adding a pinch of sugar if you like.

6 Toss the fennel and leeks in the dressing and chill. Bring the salad back to room temperature and garnish it with fennel fronds and olives before serving. Season with black pepper.

Israeli Chopped Vegetable Salad

This summery salad makes a lovely light meal when served with chunks of warm olive bread.

Serves 4–6

1 each red, green and yellow (bell) peppers, halved and seeded
1 carrot
1 cucumber
6 tomatoes
3 garlic cloves, finely chopped
3 spring onions (scallions), thinly sliced
30ml/2 tbsp chopped fresh coriander (cilantro) leaves
30ml/2 tbsp each chopped fresh dill, parsley and mint leaves
½–1 hot fresh chilli, chopped (optional)
45–60ml/3–4 tbsp extra-virgin olive oil
juice of 1–1½ lemons
salt and ground black pepper

1 Using a sharp knife, finely dice the red, green and yellow peppers, carrot, cucumber and tomatoes and place them in a large mixing bowl.

2 Add the garlic, spring onions, coriander, dill, parsley, mint and chilli, if using, to the chopped vegetables in the mixing bowl and toss together to combine.

3 Pour the olive oil and lemon juice over the vegetables, season with salt and pepper to taste and toss together. Chill for at least 1 hour before serving.

> **Cook's Tip**
> A very popular dish in Israel, this colourful salad is best made in summer when there is an abundance of fresh herbs.

> **Variation**
> This salad lends itself to endless variety: add olives, diced beetroot (beet) or potatoes, omit the chilli, vary the herbs, use lime or lemon in place of the vinegar or add a good pinch of ground cumin. It is always wonderful.

Little Onions with Coriander, Wine & Olive Oil

Packed with Mediterranean flavours, this delicious chilled dish of baby onions bathed in a piquant wine dressing makes a versatile side salad.

Serves 6
105ml/7 tbsp olive oil
675g/1½ lb small onions, peeled
150ml/¼ pint/⅔ cup dry
    white wine
2 bay leaves
2 garlic cloves, bruised
1–2 small dried red chillies
15ml/1 tbsp coriander seeds,
    toasted and lightly crushed
2.5ml/½ tsp sugar
a few fresh thyme sprigs
30ml/2 tbsp currants
10ml/2 tsp chopped fresh
    oregano or marjoram
5ml/1 tsp grated (shredded)
    lemon rind
15ml/1 tbsp chopped fresh flat
    leaf parsley
30–45ml/2–3 tbsp pine nuts,
    lightly toasted
salt and ground black pepper

1 Place 30ml/2 tbsp of the olive oil in a wide pan. Add the onions, place over a medium heat and cook gently for about 5 minutes, or until the onions begin to colour. Using a slotted spoon, transfer the onions to a dish and set aside.

2 Add the remaining oil to the pan, then stir in the wine, bay leaves, garlic, chillies, coriander seeds, sugar and thyme.

3 Bring to the boil and cook briskly for 5 minutes. Return the onions to the pan. Add the currants, reduce the heat and cook gently for 15–20 minutes, or until the onions are tender but not falling apart.

4 Using a slotted spoon, transfer the onions to a serving dish, then boil the liquid vigorously until it reduces considerably. Season with salt and pepper to taste, then pour the cooking liquid over the onions.

5 Scatter the chopped oregano or marjoram over the onions in the dish, then cool and chill. Just before serving, stir in the grated lemon rind, chopped parsley and toasted pine nuts.

Baby Leeks in Red Wine with Aromatics

Coriander seeds and oregano lend a Greek flavour to this dish of braised leeks. Serve it as part of a mixed hors d'oeuvre or as a partner for baked white fish fillets.

Serves 6
12 baby leeks or 6 thick leeks
15ml/1 tbsp coriander seeds,
    lightly crushed
5cm/2in piece cinnamon stick
120ml/4fl oz/½ cup olive oil
3 fresh bay leaves
2 strips pared orange rind
5–6 fresh or dried oregano sprigs
5ml/1 tsp caster (superfine) sugar
150ml/¼ pint/⅔ cup fruity red
    wine
10ml/2 tsp balsamic or
    sherry vinegar
30ml/2 tbsp coarsely chopped
    fresh oregano or marjoram
salt and ground black pepper

1 Leave baby leeks whole, but cut thick ones into even 5–7cm/2–3in lengths.

2 Cook the coriander seeds and cinnamon in a large pan over a medium heat for 2–3 minutes, until the spices are fragrant.

3 Stir in the oil, bay leaves, orange rind, oregano, sugar, wine and vinegar. Bring to the boil and simmer for 5 minutes.

4 Add the leeks. Bring back to the boil, reduce the heat and cover the pan. Cook gently for 5 minutes. Uncover and simmer gently for another 5–8 minutes, until the leeks are just tender when tested with the tip of a sharp knife.

5 Using a slotted spoon, transfer the leeks to a serving dish.

6 Boil the juices until they reduce to about 75–90ml/5–6 tsp. Add salt and pepper to taste and pour the reduced juices over the leeks.

7 Leave to cool, so that the flavours develop fully before serving.

Onions with coriander: Energy 227kcal/935kJ; Protein 2.5g; Carbohydrate 9.8g, of which sugars 7.2g; Fat 18.2g, of which saturates 2.2g; Cholesterol 0mg; Calcium 37mg; Fibre 1.9g; Sodium 5mg
Baby leeks: Energy 239kcal/998kJ; Protein 2.3g; Carbohydrate 7.6g, of which sugars 3g; Fat 20.5g, of which saturates 2.8g; Cholesterol 0mg; Calcium 83mg; Fibre 3.2g; Sodium 4mg

Beetroot with Fresh Mint

For adding a splash of colour to a cold spread, this ruby red salad is hard to beat. The simple mint and balsamic dressing really brings out the earthy flavour of beetroot.

Serves 4

4–6 raw beetroot (beets)
5–10ml/1–2 tsp sugar
15–30ml/1–2 tbsp balsamic
   vinegar
juice of 1/2 lemon
30ml/2 tbsp extra-virgin olive oil
1 bunch fresh mint, leaves
   stripped and thinly sliced
salt

1 Trim off the tops of the leafy stalks down to about 2.5cm/1in of the beetroot. Wash the beetroot but do not peel. Cook in boiling water for 1–2 hours, depending on the size: small ones will be tender after about 1 hour. Drain the beetroot, then cool and peel. Slice or cut into even dice with a sharp knife.

2 Put the cooked beetroot in a bowl. Add the sugar, balsamic vinegar, lemon juice, olive oil and a pinch of salt and toss together to combine.

3 Add half the thinly sliced fresh mint to the salad and toss lightly until well combined. Place the salad in the refrigerator and chill for about 1 hour. Serve garnished with the remaining thinly sliced mint leaves.

Beetroot Salad with Oranges

An unusual and delicious combination of sweet beetroot, zesty orange and warm cinnamon, this fragrant dish provides a lovely burst of colour in a summer buffet spread.

Serves 4–6

675g/1 1/2lb raw beetroot (beet)
1 orange
30ml/2 tbsp orange flower water
15ml/1 tbsp sugar
5ml/1 tsp ground cinnamon
salt and ground black pepper

1 Trim off the tops of the leafy stalks down to about 2.5cm/1in of the beetroot. Wash the beetroot but do not peel. Cook in boiling water for 1–2 hours, depending on the size: small ones will be tender after about 1 hour.

2 Meanwhile, prepare the orange. Cut a slice off the top and bottom of the orange. Place, upright, on a board and cut off the peel, working downwards with a sharp knife and taking care to remove all the bitter white pith. Turn the orange onto its side and cut into slices.

3 Drain the beetroot and leave to stand until cool enough to handle. Peel the beetroot, then cut into quarters. Cut the quarters into slices.

4 Arrange the beetroot on a plate with the orange slices, or toss them together in a bowl.

5 Gently heat the orange flower water with the sugar, stir in the cinnamon and season with salt and pepper to taste. Pour over the beetroot and orange salad and chill in the refrigerator for at least 1 hour before serving.

Cook's Tip
If you cannot find fresh beetroot (beets), or you are short of time, this salad can be successfully made with ready-cooked vacuum-packed beetroot, but pickled beetroot is not suitable as it has a vinegary flavour.

Beetroot with fresh mint: Energy 90kcal/378kJ; Protein 1.7g; Carbohydrate 8.9g, of which sugars 8.3g; Fat 5.6g, of which saturates 0.8g; Cholesterol 0mg; Calcium 21mg; Fibre 1.9g; Sodium 66mg
Beetroot salad with oranges: Energy 58kcal/247kJ; Protein 2.2g; Carbohydrate 12.9g, of which sugars 12.2g; Fat 0.1g, of which saturates 0g; Cholesterol 0mg; Calcium 33mg; Fibre 2.5g; Sodium 75mg

Beetroot & Red Onion Salad

This salad looks especially attractive when it is made with a mixture of red and yellow beetroot.

Serves 6
500g/1¼lb small raw
   beetroot (beet)
75ml/5 tbsp water
60ml/4 tbsp olive oil
90g/3½ oz/scant 1 cup
   walnut halves
5ml/1 tsp caster (superfine)
   sugar, plus a little extra for
   the dressing
30ml/2 tbsp walnut oil

15ml/1 tbsp sherry vinegar
5ml/1 tsp soy sauce
5ml/1 tsp grated (shredded)
   orange rind
2.5ml/½ tsp ground roasted
   coriander seeds
5–10ml/1–2 tsp orange juice
1 red onion, halved and very
   thinly sliced
15–30ml/1–2 tbsp chopped
   fresh fennel
75g/3oz watercress or
   mizuna leaves
handful of beetroot (beet)
   leaves (optional)
salt and ground black pepper

1 Preheat the oven to 180°C/350°F/Gas 4. Place the beetroot in an ovenproof dish in a single layer and add the water. Cover tightly and roast for 1–1½ hours, or until they are just tender.

2 Cool, then peel the beetroot. Slice or cut them into strips and toss with 15ml/1 tbsp of the olive oil in a bowl. Set aside.

3 Heat 15ml/1 tbsp of the remaining olive oil in a small frying pan. Fry the walnuts until starting to brown. Add the sugar and cook, stirring, until starting to caramelize. Season with pepper and 2.5ml/½ tsp salt, then turn them onto a plate to cool.

4 In a bowl, whisk together the remaining olive oil, the walnut oil, sherry vinegar, soy sauce, orange rind and coriander seeds. Season with salt and pepper and add a pinch of caster sugar. Whisk in orange juice to taste.

5 Separate the onion slices and add them to the beetroot. Pour over the dressing and toss well. Just before serving, toss with the fennel, watercress and beetroot leaves, if using. Transfer to individual plates and sprinkle with the caramelized nuts.

Beetroot with Lemon Dressing

Fresh beetroot has a lovely, sweet, earthy flavour which is beautifully enhanced with this simple lemon dressing. The subtle taste of freshly cooked beetroot is a far cry from commercially sold pickled beetroot.

Serves 4
450g/1lb raw beetroot (beets)
grated (shredded) rind and juice
   of ½ lemon
about 150ml/¼ pint/⅔ cup
   extra-virgin olive oil (or a
   mixture of olive and sunflower
   oil, blended to taste)
sea salt and ground black pepper
chopped fresh chives,
   to garnish

1 Trim off the tops of the leafy stalks down to about 2.5cm/1in of the beetroot. Wash the beetroot but do not peel.

2 Cook in boiling water for 1–2 hours, depending on the size; small ones will be tender after about 1 hour.

3 Drain the beetroot and, when cool enough to handle, remove the skin, which will come away easily. Leave until completely cool.

4 Peel when cool and slice into wedges into a bowl. Add the lemon rind and juice, and the oil; season to taste. Mix the dressing in gently and serve.

Beetroot & red onion salad: Energy 238kcal/986kJ; Protein 3.8g; Carbohydrate 8g, of which sugars 7.4g; Fat 21.4g, of which saturates 2.2g; Cholesterol 0mg; Calcium 36mg; Fibre 2.3g; Sodium 116mg
Beetroot with lemon dressing: Energy 265kcal/1097kJ; Protein 1.9g; Carbohydrate 8.6g, of which sugars 7.9g; Fat 25.1g, of which saturates 3.6g; Cholesterol 0mg; Calcium 23mg; Fibre 2.2g; Sodium 74mg

Lamb's Lettuce & Beetroot

This salad makes a colourful and unusual starter – the delicate flavour of the lamb's lettuce is perfect with the earthiness of the beetroot. For extra texture, sprinkle with chopped walnuts.

Serves 4
150–175g/5–6oz/3–4 cups
  lamb's lettuce (corn salad),
  washed and roots trimmed
250g/9oz/3 or 4 small fresh
  beetroot (beets), cooked,
  peeled and diced
30ml/2 tbsp chopped
  fresh parsley

For the vinaigrette
30–45ml/2–3 tbsp white wine
  vinegar or lemon juice
20ml/4 tsp Dijon mustard
2 garlic cloves, finely chopped
2.5ml/½ tsp sugar
120ml/4fl oz/½ cup sunflower or
  grapeseed oil
120ml/4fl oz/½ cup crème
  fraîche or double (heavy) cream
salt and ground black pepper

1 First make the vinaigrette. Mix the vinegar or lemon juice, mustard, garlic and sugar in a small bowl. Season with salt and pepper, then slowly whisk in the oil until the sauce thickens.

2 Lightly beat the crème fraîche or double cream to lighten it slightly, then whisk it into the dressing.

3 Toss the lettuce with a little of the vinaigrette and arrange on a serving plate or in a bowl.

4 Spoon the beetroot into the centre of the lettuce and drizzle over the remaining vinaigrette.

5 Sprinkle with chopped parsley and serve immediately.

Cook's Tip
To cook fresh beetroot (beet), place unpeeled in a roasting pan with 1cm/½in water and roast in a medium oven for about an hour until tender. Allow to cool slightly before peeling.

Turnip Salad in Soured Cream

This tangy salad partners cheese dishes extremely well, and it makes an interesting addition to a selection of salads. Only very young, tender turnips should be used.

Serves 4
2–4 young, tender turnips, peeled
¼–½ onion, finely chopped
2–3 drops white wine vinegar, or
  to taste
60–90ml/4–6 tbsp soured cream
salt and ground black pepper
chopped fresh parsley or paprika,
  to garnish

1 Thinly slice or coarsely grate (shred) the turnips. Alternatively, thinly slice half the turnips and grate the remaining half. Place in a serving bowl.

2 Add the onion, vinegar and salt and pepper to taste. Toss together then stir in the soured cream.

3 Serve chilled, garnished with a sprinkling of parsley or paprika.

Variations
• *Crème fraîche can be used instead of the sour cream.*
• *When young turnips are not available, try using the dressing with sliced radishes instead, and replace the onion with spring onions (scallions) or snipped chives.*

Lamb's lettuce & beetroot: Energy 329kcal/1360kJ; Protein 2.7g; Carbohydrate 7.5g, of which sugars 6.9g; Fat 32.3g, of which saturates 10.5g; Cholesterol 34mg; Calcium 64mg; Fibre 2g; Sodium 200mg
Turnip salad: Energy 48kcal/198kJ; Protein 1.1g; Carbohydrate 4.1g, of which sugars 3.7g; Fat 3.2g, of which saturates 1.9g; Cholesterol 9mg; Calcium 42mg; Fibre 1.4g; Sodium 14mg

Potato Salad with Capers & Black Olives

A dish from southern Italy, the combination of olives, capers and anchovies is quite perfect.

Serves 4–6
900g/2lb large white potatoes
50ml/2fl oz/¼ cup white
    wine vinegar
75ml/5 tbsp olive oil
30ml/2 tbsp chopped flat
    leaf parsley

30ml/2 tbsp capers, finely
    chopped
50g/2oz/½ cup pitted black
    olives, chopped in half
3 garlic cloves, finely chopped
50g/2oz marinated anchovies
    (unsalted)
salt and ground black pepper

1 Boil the potatoes in their skins in a large pan for 20 minutes or until just tender. Remove from the pan using a slotted spoon and place them in a separate bowl.

2 When the potatoes are cool enough to handle, carefully peel off the skins.

3 Cut the peeled potatoes into even chunks and place in a large, flat earthenware dish.

4 Mix together the vinegar and oil, season to taste and add the parsley, capers, olives and garlic. Toss carefully to combine and then pour over the potato chunks.

5 Lay the anchovies on top of the salad. Cover with a cloth and leave the salad to settle for 30 minutes or so before serving to allow the flavours to penetrate.

> **Variation**
> If you want to serve this dish to vegetarians, simply omit the anchovies, it tastes delicious even without them.

Potatoes with Egg & Lemon Dressing

This old favourite takes on a new lease of life when mixed with hard-boiled eggs and lemon juice. With its tangy flavour, it is the ideal salad to accompany a summer barbecue.

Serves 4
900g/2lb new potatoes
1 small onion, finely chopped

2 hard-boiled (hard-cooked)
    eggs, shelled
300ml/½ pint/1¼ cups
    mayonnaise
1 garlic clove, crushed
finely grated (shredded) rind and
    juice of 1 lemon
60ml/4 tbsp chopped fresh
    parsley, plus extra
    for garnishing
salt and ground black pepper

1 Scrub or scrape the potatoes. Put them in a pan, cover with cold water and add a pinch of salt. Bring to the boil, then simmer for 15 minutes, or until tender. Drain and allow to cool. Cut the potatoes into large dice, season well with salt and pepper and combine with the chopped onion.

2 Halve the eggs and set aside the yolk. Roughly chop the whites and place in a mixing bowl. Stir in the mayonnaise. Mix the garlic, lemon rind and lemon juice in a small bowl and stir into the mayonnaise mixture, combining thoroughly.

3 Stir the mayonnaise mixture into the potatoes, coating them well, then fold in the chopped parsley. Press the egg yolk through a sieve (strainer) and sprinkle on top. Serve cold or chilled, garnished with parsley.

> **Variation**
> For a change, replace the potato with cooked beetroot (beet). The mayonnaise will turn bright pink, which may surprise your guests, but the flavour is excellent. Alternatively, use a mixture of potatoes and beetroot.

Potato salad: Energy 282kcal/1174kJ; Protein 5g; Carbohydrate 24.4g, of which sugars 2.2g; Fat 18.9g, of which saturates 2.8g; Cholesterol 5mg; Calcium 54mg; Fibre 2g; Sodium 347mg
Potatoes with egg & lemon dressing: Energy 723kcal/3000kJ; Protein 8.4g; Carbohydrate 39.1g, of which sugars 5.1g; Fat 60.4g, of which saturates 9.6g; Cholesterol 151mg; Calcium 68mg; Fibre 3.2g; Sodium 403mg

Fiery Cajun Potato Salad

Tabasco sauce gives this salad a punchy flavour.

Serves 6–8

8 waxy potatoes
1 green (bell) pepper, seeded and diced
1 large gherkin, chopped
4 spring onions (scallions), shredded
3 hard-boiled (hard-cooked) eggs, shelled and chopped
250ml/8fl oz/1 cup mayonnaise
15ml/1 tbsp Dijon mustard
salt and ground black pepper
Tabasco sauce, to taste
1–2 pinches cayenne pepper
sliced gherkin, to garnish
mayonnaise, to serve

1 Cook the potatoes in their skins in a large pan of salted boiling water until tender. Drain well and leave to cool.

2 When the potatoes are cool enough to handle, peel them and cut into coarse chunks. Transfer the potatoes to a large bowl and add the green pepper, gherkin, spring onions and hard-boiled eggs. Toss gently to mix.

3 In a separate bowl, mix the mayonnaise with the mustard and season with salt, black pepper and Tabasco sauce to taste.

4 Toss the dressing into the potato mixture and sprinkle with a pinch or two of cayenne. Serve the salad with mayonnaise and a garnish of sliced gherkin.

Deli Potato Salad with Olives

Potato salad is synonymous with deli food and there are many varieties, some with soured cream, some with vinaigrette and others with vegetables. This tasty version includes a piquant mustard mayonnaise, chopped eggs and green olives.

Serves 6–8

1kg/2¼lb waxy salad potatoes, scrubbed
1 red, brown or white onion, finely chopped
2–3 celery sticks, finely chopped
60–90ml/4–6 tbsp chopped fresh parsley
15–20 pimiento-stuffed olives, halved
3 hard-boiled (hard-cooked) eggs, chopped
60ml/4 tbsp extra virgin olive oil
60ml/4 tbsp white wine vinegar
15–30ml/1–2 tbsp mild or wholegrain mustard
celery seeds, to taste (optional)
175–250ml/6–8fl oz/¾–1 cup mayonnaise
salt and ground black pepper
paprika, to garnish

1 Put the potatoes in a pan, pour in water to cover and add a pinch of salt. Bring to the boil, then reduce the heat and cook gently for about 10 minutes, or until the potatoes are just tender. Drain well and return to the pan. Leave for 2–3 minutes to cool and dry a little.

2 When the potatoes are cool enough to handle but still very warm, cut them with a sharp knife into chunks or slices and place in a salad bowl.

3 Sprinkle the potatoes with salt and ground black pepper, then add the onion, celery, parsley, olives and the chopped eggs.

4 Place the olive oil in a small bowl, then whisk in the vinegar, mustard and celery seeds, if using. Pour the dressing over the salad and toss to combine.

5 Stir in enough mayonnaise to bind the salad together. Chill before serving, sprinkled with a little paprika.

Fiery Cajun potato salad: Energy 289kcal/1197kJ; Protein 4g; Carbohydrate 10.3g, of which sugars 2.7g; Fat 26.1g, of which saturates 4.2g; Cholesterol 95mg; Calcium 21mg; Fibre 0.9g; Sodium 229mg
Deli potato salad: Energy 323kcal/1343kJ; Protein 5.2g; Carbohydrate 21.5g, of which sugars 2.7g; Fat 24.7g, of which saturates 4g; Cholesterol 88mg; Calcium 49mg; Fibre 2g; Sodium 149mg

Potato & Olive Salad

This delicious version of potato salad is simple and zesty – perfect as a quick and easy side salad.

Serves 4

8 large new potatoes
45–60ml/3–4 tbsp
  garlic-flavoured oil and
  vinegar dressing
60–90ml/4–6 tbsp chopped fresh
  herbs, such as coriander
  (cilantro) and chives
10–15 dry-fleshed black
  Mediterranean olives
pinch of ground cumin, to garnish

1 Cut the new potatoes into chunks. Put them in a pan, pour in water to cover and add a pinch of salt. Bring to the boil, then reduce the heat and cook gently for about 10 minutes, or until the potatoes are just tender. Drain well and leave in a colander to dry thoroughly and cool slightly.

2 When the potatoes are cool enough to handle, chop them and put in a serving bowl.

3 Drizzle the garlic-flavoured dressing over the potatoes. Toss well together, then sprinkle with the chopped fresh herbs and black olives.

4 Chill in the refrigerator for at least 1 hour before serving. Serve garnished with a little ground cumin.

> **Cook's Tip**
> *Similar in appearance to flat leaf parsley, fresh coriander (cilantro) has a distinctive pungent, almost spicy flavour that makes a delicious addition to salads. It is widely used in India, the Middle and Far East and in many eastern Mediterranean countries.*

Potato, Caraway Seed & Parsley Salad

Leaving the potatoes to cool in garlic-infused oil with the caraway seeds helps them to absorb plenty of flavour.

Serves 4–6

675g/1½lb new potatoes,
  scrubbed
45ml/3 tbsp garlic-infused olive oil
15ml/1 tbsp caraway seeds,
  lightly crushed
45ml/3 tbsp chopped fresh
  parsley
salt and ground black pepper

1 Cook the potatoes in salted, boiling water for about 10 minutes, or until just tender. Drain thoroughly and transfer to a large bowl.

2 Stir the oil, caraway seeds and some salt and pepper into the hot potatoes, then set aside to cool. When the potatoes are almost cold, stir in the parsley and serve.

Spicy Potato Salad

This tasty salad is quick to prepare, and makes a satisfying accompaniment to plainly cooked meat or fish.

Serves 6

900g/2lb potatoes
2 red (bell) peppers, seeded
  and diced
2 celery sticks, finely chopped
1 shallot, finely chopped
2 or 3 spring onions (scallions),
  finely chopped
1 green chilli, seeded and
  finely chopped
1 garlic clove, crushed
10ml/2 tsp finely snipped
  fresh chives
10ml/2 tsp finely chopped
  fresh basil
15ml/1 tbsp finely chopped
  fresh parsley
15ml/1 tbsp single (light) cream
30ml/2 tbsp salad cream
15ml/1 tbsp mayonnaise
5ml/1 tsp prepared mild mustard
7.5ml/1½ tsp sugar
salt
snipped fresh chives, to garnish

1 Peel the potatoes. Boil in salted water for 10–12 minutes, until tender. Drain and cool, then cut into cubes and place in a large mixing bowl.

2 Add chopped red peppers, celery, shallot, spring onions and green chilli to the potatoes, together with the crushed garlic and chopped herbs, and stir gently to combine.

3 To make the dressing, blend the cream, salad cream, mayonnaise, mustard and sugar in a small bowl, stirring until the mixture is well combined.

4 Pour the dressing over the salad and toss gently to coat evenly. Serve garnished with the snipped chives.

> **Variations**
> *If you prefer, leave out the salad cream and increase the amount of mayonnaise by 30ml/2 tbsp. To turn the salad into a light lunch dish, add some diced ham and a handful of cooked green beans that have been refreshed under cold running water.*

Potato & olive salad: Energy 132kcal/548kJ; Protein 1.8g; Carbohydrate 12.4g, of which sugars 1.2g; Fat 8.6g, of which saturates 1.3g; Cholesterol 0mg; Calcium 42mg; Fibre 2.1g; Sodium 575mg
Potato, caraway seed & parsley salad: Energy 131kcal/549kJ; Protein 2.1g; Carbohydrate 18.3g, of which sugars 1.6g; Fat 5.9g, of which saturates 0.9g; Cholesterol 0mg; Calcium 22mg; Fibre 1.5g; Sodium 15mg
Spicy potato salad: Energy 178kcal/749kJ; Protein 3.9g; Carbohydrate 31.4g, of which sugars 8.7g; Fat 4.9g, of which saturates 1g; Cholesterol 5mg; Calcium 48mg; Fibre 3.3g; Sodium 118mg

Potato & Radish Salad

Radishes add a splash of crunch and peppery flavour to this honey-scented salad. So many potato salads are dressed in a thick sauce. This one, however, is quite light and colourful with a tasty yet delicate dressing.

Serves 4–6
450g/1lb new or salad potatoes
45ml/3 tbsp olive oil
15ml/1 tbsp walnut or hazelnut oil (optional)
30ml/2 tbsp wine vinegar
10ml/2 tsp coarse-grain mustard
5ml/1 tsp honey
about 6–8 radishes, thinly sliced
30ml/2 tbsp snipped chives
salt and ground black pepper

1 Cook the potatoes in their skins in a large pan of boiling salted water until just tender. Drain well and leave to cool slightly. When cool enough to handle, cut the potatoes in half, but leave any small ones whole. Place in a large bowl.

2 To make the dressing, place the oils, vinegar, mustard and honey in a bowl and season to taste with salt and pepper. Whisk together until thoroughly combined.

3 Toss the dressing into the potatoes in the bowl while they are still cooling and leave to stand for 1–2 hours to allow the flavours to penetrate.

4 Finally, mix in the sliced radishes and snipped chives and chill in the refrigerator until ready to serve.

5 Just before serving, toss the salad mixture together again, as some of the dressing may have settled on the bottom, and adjust the seasoning.

Variation
Sliced celery stick, diced red onion and/or chopped walnuts would make good alternatives to the radishes if you are unable to get hold of any.

Tangy Potato Salad

If you like a good kick of mustard and the distinctive flavour of tarragon, you'll love this combination.

Serves 8
1.3kg/3lb small new or salad potatoes
30ml/2 tbsp white wine vinegar
15ml/1 tbsp Dijon mustard
45ml/3 tbsp vegetable or olive oil
75g/3oz/6 tbsp chopped red onion
120ml/4fl oz/½ cup mayonnaise
30ml/2 tbsp chopped fresh tarragon, or 7.5ml/1½ tsp dried tarragon
1 celery stick, thinly sliced
salt and ground black pepper
celery leaves and tarragon leaves, to garnish

1 Cook the potatoes in their skins in boiling salted water for about 15–20 minutes until tender. Drain well.

2 Mix together the vinegar and Dijon mustard, then slowly whisk in the oil.

3 When the potatoes are cool enough to handle, slice them into a large bowl. Add the onion to the potatoes, then pour the dressing over them. Season with salt and pepper to taste, then toss gently to combine. Leave to stand for at least 30 minutes.

4 Mix together the mayonnaise and tarragon. Gently stir into the potatoes, together with the celery. Serve garnished with celery leaves and tarragon.

Cook's Tip
The delicious, distinctive tarragon flavour in this dish makes it the perfect partner to roast or grilled (broiled) chicken.

Variation
When available, use small red or even blue potatoes to give an interesting colour to the salad.

Vegetable Gado-Gado Salad with Peanut Sambal

This classic Indonesian salad combines lightly steamed vegetables and hard-boiled eggs with a richly flavoured peanut dressing.

Serves 6
225g/8oz new potatoes, halved
2 carrots, cut into sticks
115g/4oz green beans
½ small cauliflower, broken
  into florets
¼ firm white cabbage, shredded
200g/7oz bean or lentil sprouts
4 eggs, hard-boiled (hard-cooked)
  and quartered
bunch of watercress (optional)

For the sauce
90ml/6 tbsp crunchy
  peanut butter
300ml/½ pint/1¼ cups
  cold water
1 garlic clove, crushed
30ml/2 tbsp dark soy sauce
15ml/1 tbsp dry sherry
10ml/2 tsp caster
  (superfine) sugar
15ml/1 tbsp fresh lemon juice

1 Place the halved potatoes in a metal colander or steamer and set over a pan of gently boiling water. Cover the pan or steamer with a lid and cook the potatoes for 10 minutes.

2 Add the rest of the vegetables to the steamer and steam for a further 10 minutes, until tender. Cool and arrange on a platter with the egg quarters and the watercress, if using.

3 Beat together all the ingredients for the sauce in a large mixing bowl until smooth. Drizzle a little sauce over the salad then pour the rest into a small bowl and serve separately.

> **Variation**
> *There are a range of nut butters available in supermarkets and health-food stores. Try using hazelnut, almond or cashew nut butter in place of peanut butter to create a milder sauce.*

Artichoke Heart & Orange Salad

Fresh artichoke hearts are combined with citrus fruit, radishes and black olives to create a colourful salad that will please the eye and refresh the palate – perfect to serve alongside, or after, a spicy dish.

Serves 4
1 lemon, halved
4 artichoke hearts
4 Seville (Temple) oranges
6 red radishes, finely sliced
12 kalamata olives
30–45ml/2–3 tbsp olive oil
salt
2.5ml/½ tsp paprika, to serve

1 Squeeze the juice from ½ lemon and pour into a pan. Add the artichoke hearts and plenty of water to cover. Bring to the boil, then reduce the heat and simmer gently for about 15 minutes until just tender.

2 Drain and refresh the hearts under cold running water, then drain again. Slice the artichoke hearts thickly and place them in a mixing bowl.

3 Peel the oranges with a sharp knife, cutting off all the pith. Cut between the membranes to remove the segments of fruit. Discard any pips and add the segments to the artichoke hearts.

4 Add the radishes and olives, drizzle with the olive oil and the juice from the remaining ½ lemon, and carefully mix together. Season with salt, sprinkle with a little paprika and serve.

> **Cook's Tips**
> *• To prepare the artichoke hearts for cooking, remove the leaves from whole fresh artichokes. Cut off the stems, scoop out the choke and hairy bits, and immerse them in water mixed with a squeeze of lemon juice.*
> *• When fresh artichokes are not readily available, opt for the frozen hearts that can be found in some supermarkets.*
> *• You can use sweet or sour Seville oranges for this dish. When Sevilles are out of season, use any large, juicy variety.*

Vegetable gado-gado: Energy 199kcal/831kJ; Protein 10.5g; Carbohydrate 14g, of which sugars 6.6g; Fat 11.3g, of which saturates 2.9g; Cholesterol 127mg; Calcium 58mg; Fibre 3.1g; Sodium 819mg
Artichoke heart & orange salad: Energy 243kcal/1007kJ; Protein 2.1g; Carbohydrate 12g, of which sugars 12g; Fat 21.1g, of which saturates 3g; Cholesterol 0mg; Calcium 112mg; Fibre 3.6g; Sodium 83mg

Globe Artichoke Salad

This salad first course is a great way to make the most of artichokes. It is equally good served hot or cold.

Serves 4

4 artichokes
juice of 1 lemon
900ml/1½ pints/3¾ cups
    home-made vegetable stock
    and water mixed
2 garlic cloves, chopped
1 small bunch parsley
6 whole peppercorns
15ml/1 tbsp olive oil, plus
    extra for drizzling

1 To prepare the artichokes, trim the stalks of the artichokes close to the base, cut the very tips off the leaves and then divide them into quarters. Remove the inedible hairy choke (the central part), carefully scraping the hairs away from the heart at the base of the artichoke.

2 Squeeze a little of the lemon juice over the cut surfaces of the artichokes to prevent discoloration.

3 Put the artichokes into a pan and cover with the stock and water, garlic, parsley, peppercorns and olive oil. Cover with a lid and cook gently for 1 hour, or until the artichokes are tender. They are ready when the leaves come away easily when pulled. Remove the artichokes with a slotted spoon. Boil the cooking liquid hard to reduce by half, then strain.

4 To serve, arrange the artichokes in small serving dishes and pour over the reduced juices. Drizzle over a little extra olive oil and lemon juice. Provide finger bowls and a bowl for the leaves.

5 To eat, pull a leaf away from the artichoke and scrape the fleshy part at the base with your teeth. Discard the remainder of the leaves and then eat the heart at the base.

Variation
If you can find tiny purple artichokes with tapered leaves, they can be cooked and eaten whole as the chokes are very tender.

Californian Salad

Full of vitality and vitamins, this is a lovely light and healthy salad for sunny summer days.

Serves 4

1 small crisp lettuce, torn
    into pieces
225g/8oz/4 cups young
    spinach leaves
2 carrots, coarsely grated
115g/4oz cherry tomatoes,
    halved
2 celery sticks, thinly sliced
75g/3oz/½ cup raisins
50g/2oz/½ cup blanched
    almonds or unsalted cashew
    nuts, halved
30ml/2 tbsp sunflower seeds
30ml/2 tbsp sesame seeds,
    lightly toasted

For the dressing
45ml/3 tbsp extra virgin olive oil
30ml/2 tbsp cider vinegar
10ml/2 tsp clear honey
juice of 1 small orange
salt and ground black pepper

1 Put the lettuce, spinach, carrots, tomatoes and celery in a large bowl. Add the raisins, almonds and the sunflower and sesame seeds.

2 Put all the dressing ingredients in a screw-top jar and shake well to combine, then pour over the salad.

3 Toss the salad thoroughly and divide among four small salad bowls. Season with salt and pepper and serve immediately.

Cook's Tips
• *For tomato and mozzarella toasts to serve with the salad, cut French bread diagonally into slices, then toast lightly on both sides. Spread some sun-dried tomato paste on one side of each slice. Cut some mozzarella into small pieces and arrange over the tomato paste. Put on baking sheets, sprinkle with chopped herbs and black pepper to taste and drizzle with olive oil. Bake in a hot oven for 5 minutes or until the mozzarella has melted. Leave to settle for a few minutes before serving.*
• *If the tomatoes are hard and tasteless, try roasting them in the oven with a little olive oil, then add to the salad.*

Globe artichoke salad: Energy 59kcal/245kJ; Protein 0.7g; Carbohydrate 7.8g, of which sugars 7.3g; Fat 3.1g, of which saturates 0.5g; Cholesterol 0mg; Calcium 25mg; Fibre 2.4g; Sodium 61mg
Californian salad: Energy 319kcal/1327kJ; Protein 7.9g; Carbohydrate 23.5g, of which sugars 21.7g; Fat 22.1g, of which saturates 2.6g; Cholesterol 0mg; Calcium 205mg; Fibre 5g; Sodium 114mg.

Cabbage Salad with Lemon Dressing & Black Olives

During the winter in Greece, this *lahano salata* frequently appears on the meal table. Traditionally made with compact creamy-coloured "white" cabbage, it has a lovely crisp texture.

Serves 4

1 white cabbage
12 black olives

For the dressing

75–90ml/5–6 tbsp extra-virgin
    olive oil
30ml/2 tbsp lemon juice
1 garlic clove, crushed
30ml/2 tbsp finely chopped fresh
    flat leaf parsley
salt

1 Cut the cabbage in quarters, discard the outer leaves and trim off any thick, hard stems as well as the hard base.

2 Lay each quarter in turn on its side and cut long, very thin slices until you reach the central core, which should be discarded. Place the cabbage in a bowl and stir in the olives.

3 To make the dressing, whisk the extra-virgin olive oil, lemon juice, garlic, chopped parsley and salt together in a bowl until well blended.

4 Pour the dressing over the cabbage and olives, and toss the salad until evenly coated. Serve immediately.

Cook's Tips
• *The key to a perfect cabbage salad is to choose a very fresh, crisp cabbage and shred it as finely as possible; use a large, very sharp knife.*
• *Add shredded raw carrot and toasted pine nuts for variety.*
• *You can prepare the cabbage ahead of time and keep it fresh in a bowl of cold water. When you are ready, drain the cabbage and quickly assemble the salad.*

Gingered Carrot Salad

This fresh and zesty salad is ideal served as an accompaniment to simple grilled chicken or fish. Fresh root ginger goes perfectly with sweet carrots, and the tiny black poppy seeds not only add taste and texture, but also look stunning against the bright orange of the carrots.

Serves 4

350g/12oz carrots
30ml/2 tbsp garlic-infused olive oil
2.5cm/1in piece of fresh root
    ginger, peeled and grated
    (shredded)
15ml/1 tbsp poppy seeds
salt and ground black pepper

1 Peel the carrots and cut them into fine matchsticks. Put them in a bowl and stir in the oil and grated ginger. Cover and chill for at least 30 minutes, to allow the flavours to develop fully.

2 Season the salad with salt and pepper to taste. Stir in the poppy seeds just before serving.

Cook's Tips
• *Some food processors have an attachment that can be used to cut the carrots into batons, which makes quick work of the preparation, but even cutting them by hand doesn't take long.*
• *It is best to use organic carrots for the best flavour, or at least carrots with their green tops still attached.*
• *You can always use another type of flavoured oil, such as chilli oil, or even use extra-virgin olive oil and add a little chopped fresh coriander (cilantro) or chives to the salad.*

Variation
To make a parsnip and sesame seed salad, replace the carrots with parsnips and blanch in boiling salted water for 1 minute before combining with the oil and ginger. Replace the poppy seeds with the same quantity of sesame seeds.

Cabbage salad: Energy 307kcal/1269kJ; Protein 3.9g; Carbohydrate 12.8g, of which sugars 12.5g; Fat 26.9g, of which saturates 3.8g; Cholesterol 0mg; Calcium 145mg; Fibre 5.8g; Sodium 21mg
Gingered carrot salad: Energy 103kcal/424kJ; Protein 1.2g; Carbohydrate 7g, of which sugars 6.5g; Fat 7.9g, of which saturates 1.2g; Cholesterol 0mg; Calcium 47mg; Fibre 2.4g; Sodium 23mg

Coleslaw with Pesto Mayonnaise

Fennel Coleslaw

Basil-flavoured pesto gives this coleslaw a deliciously different taste.

Serves 4–6
1 small or ½ medium
  white cabbage
3–4 carrots, grated
4 spring onions (scallions),
  finely sliced
25–40g/1–1½oz/¼–⅓ cup
  pine nuts

15ml/1 tbsp chopped or torn
  fresh mixed herbs such as
  parsley, basil and chervil

For the pesto mayonnaise
1 egg yolk
about 10ml/2tsp lemon juice
200ml/7fl oz/scant 1 cup
  sunflower oil
10ml/2 tsp pesto
60ml/4 tbsp natural (plain) yogurt
salt and ground black pepper

1 To make the mayonnaise, place the egg yolk in a blender or food processor and process with the lemon juice. With the machine running, very slowly add the oil, pouring it more quickly as the mayonnaise emulsifies.

2 Season to taste with salt and pepper and a little more lemon juice if necessary. (Alternatively, make the mayonnaise by hand using a balloon whisk.) Spoon 75ml/5 tbsp of the mayonnaise into a bowl and stir in the pesto and yogurt, beating well to make a fairly thin dressing.

3 Remove the outer leaves of the cabbage and discard. Using a food processor or a sharp knife, thinly slice the cabbage and place in a large salad bowl.

4 Add the carrots and spring onions, together with the pine nuts and herbs, mixing thoroughly with your hands. Stir the pesto dressing into the salad or serve separately in a small dish.

> **Cook's Tip**
> If you are short of time, you can use ready-made mayonnaise with just as much success. Add the dressing just before serving to keep the cabbage crisp.

Another variation on traditional coleslaw in which the aniseed flavour of fennel plays a major role.

Serves 4
175g/6oz fennel
2 spring onions (scallions)
175g/6oz white cabbage
115g/4oz celery
175g/6oz carrots

50g/2oz/scant ½ cup sultanas
  (golden raisins)
2.5ml/½ tsp caraway seeds
  (optional)
15ml/1 tbsp chopped fresh
  parsley
45ml/3 tbsp extra-virgin olive oil
5ml/1 tsp lemon juice
strips of spring onion (scallion),
  to garnish

1 Using a sharp knife, cut the fennel and spring onions into thin slices. Place in a serving bowl.

2 Slice the cabbage and celery finely and cut the carrots into fine strips. Add to the fennel and spring onions in the serving bowl. Add the sultanas and caraway seeds, if using, and toss lightly to mix through.

3 Stir in the chopped parsley, olive oil and lemon juice and mix all the ingredients very thoroughly.

4 Cover and chill for 3 hours to allow the flavours to mingle. Serve garnished with strips of spring onion.

Coleslaw with pesto mayonnaise: Energy 292kcal/1202kJ; Protein 2.7g; Carbohydrate 5.1g, of which sugars 5g; Fat 29g, of which saturates 3.5g; Cholesterol 34mg; Calcium 61mg; Fibre 1.8g; Sodium 17mg
Fennel coleslaw: Energy 145kcal/604kJ; Protein 1.9g; Carbohydrate 15.6g, of which sugars 15.3g; Fat 8.7g, of which saturates 1.2g; Cholesterol 0mg; Calcium 70mg; Fibre 3.8g; Sodium 46mg

Curried Red Cabbage Slaw

A variation on a Jewish favourite, this spicy coleslaw is excellent for adding flavour and colour to a cold meal. Quick and easy to make, it is a useful dish for a last-minute gathering.

Serves 4–6
1/2 red cabbage, thinly sliced
1 red (bell) pepper, chopped or very thinly sliced
1/2 red onion, chopped
60ml/4 tbsp red, white wine vinegar or cider vinegar
60ml/4 tbsp sugar, or to taste
120ml/4fl oz/1/2 cup Greek (US strained plain) yogurt or natural (plain) yogurt
120ml/4fl oz/1/2 cup mayonnaise, preferably home-made
1.5ml/1/4 tsp curry powder
2–3 handfuls of raisins
salt and ground black pepper

1 Put the cabbage, red pepper and red onions in a bowl and toss to combine thoroughly.

2 Heat the vinegar and sugar in a small pan until the sugar has dissolved, then pour over the vegetables. Leave to cool slightly.

3 Mix together the yogurt and mayonnaise, then stir into the cabbage mixture. Season to taste with curry powder, salt and ground black pepper, then mix in the raisins.

4 Chill the salad for at least 2 hours before serving. Just before serving, drain off any excess liquid and briefly stir the slaw again.

> **Cook's Tip**
> If you have time, it is worth making your own mayonnaise.

> **Variation**
> • To make a tangy pareve slaw, suitable for serving with a meat meal, omit the natural (plain) yogurt and mayonnaise and add a little more vinegar.

Raw Vegetable Yam

In Thai cooking, yam dishes are salads made with raw or lightly cooked vegetables, dressed with a special spicy sauce. They are a real treat.

Serves 4
50g/2oz watercress or baby spinach, chopped
1/2 cucumber, finely diced
2 celery sticks, finely diced
2 carrots, finely diced
1 red (bell) pepper, seeded and finely diced
2 tomatoes, seeded and finely diced
small bunch fresh mint, chopped
90g/3 1/2oz cellophane noodles

For the yam
2 small fresh red chillies, seeded and finely chopped
60ml/4 tbsp light soy sauce
45ml/3 tbsp lemon juice
5ml/1 tsp palm sugar (jaggery) or light muscovado (brown) sugar
60ml/4 tbsp water
1 head pickled garlic, finely chopped, plus 15ml/1 tbsp vinegar from the jar
50g/2oz/scant 1/2 cup peanuts, roasted and chopped
90g/3 1/2oz fried tofu, finely chopped
15ml/1 tbsp sesame seeds, toasted

1 Place the watercress or spinach leaves, diced cucumber, celery, carrots, red pepper and tomatoes in a serving bowl. Add the chopped mint and toss all the ingredients together using clean hands.

2 Soak the noodles in boiling water for 3 minutes, or according to the packet instructions, then drain well and snip with scissors into shorter lengths. Add the softened noodles to the vegetables.

3 To make the yam, put the chopped chillies in a pan and add the soy sauce, lemon juice, sugar and water. Place over a medium heat and stir until the sugar has dissolved.

4 Add the garlic, with the pickling vinegar from the jar, then mix in the chopped nuts, tofu and toasted sesame seeds.

5 Pour the yam over the vegetables and noodles, toss together until well mixed, and serve immediately.

Curried red cabbage slaw: Energy 286kcal/1194kJ; Protein 3.5g; Carbohydrate 31.6g, of which sugars 31g; Fat 17g, of which saturates 2.6g; Cholesterol 17mg; Calcium 108mg; Fibre 3.1g; Sodium 134mg
Raw vegetable yam: Energy 276kcal/1152kJ; Protein 12.1g; Carbohydrate 28.8g, of which sugars 9g; Fat 12.4g, of which saturates 1.5g; Cholesterol 0mg; Calcium 415mg; Fibre 3.1g; Sodium 1101mg

Lotus Stem Salad with Shallots & Shredded Fresh Basil

In this exotic Vietnamese-style salad, lotus stems absorb the flavours of the dressing while retaining a crunchy texture.

Serves 4
½ cucumber
225g/8oz jar preserved lotus stems, drained and cut into 5cm/2in strips
2 shallots, finely sliced

25g/1oz/½ cup fresh basil leaves, shredded
fresh coriander (cilantro) leaves, to garnish

For the dressing
juice of 1 lime
15–30ml/1–2 tbsp nuoc mam
1 red Thai chilli, seeded and finely chopped
1 garlic clove, crushed
15ml/1 tbsp sugar

1 To make the dressing, mix together the dressing ingredients in a bowl and set aside.

2 Peel the cucumber and cut it into thin 5cm/2in strips. Soak the strips in cold salted water for 20 minutes.

3 Put the lotus stems into a bowl of water. Using a pair of chopsticks, stir the water constantly so that the loose fibres of the stems wrap around the sticks. Drain the stems and put them in a bowl.

4 Drain the cucumber strips and add them to the bowl, then add the shallots, shredded basil leaves and the prepared dressing. Leave the salad to marinate for 20 minutes before serving. Garnish with fresh coriander leaves.

Cook's Tip
You may be lucky enough to find fresh lotus stems in an Asian market, but the ones preserved in brine are perfectly adequate for this recipe. Fresh lotus roots can also be used: peel and soak in water with a little lemon juice before adding to the salad.

Pickled Broccoli & Cucumber

Broccoli stem is usually wasted because of the fibrous texture, but you will be surprised how tasty it is when marinated or pickled. In this recipe, miso and garlic give a kick to its subtle flavour. The pickle, which will keep for a few days, also makes a good accompaniment to drinks.

Serves 4
3 broccoli stems (use the florets in another dish, if you wish)
2 Japanese or salad cucumbers, ends trimmed
200ml/7fl oz/scant 1 cup miso (any kind)
15ml/1 tbsp sake
1 garlic clove, crushed

1 Peel the broccoli stems and quarter them lengthways. With a vegetable peeler, peel the cucumber every 5mm/¼in to make green-and-white stripes. Cut in half lengthways. Scoop out the centre with a teaspoon. Cut into 7.5cm/3in lengths.

2 Mix the miso, sake and crushed garlic in a deep, plastic or metal container with a lid. Remove half the miso mix.

3 Lay some of the broccoli stems and cucumber flat in the container and push into the miso mix. Spread a little of the reserved miso over the top of the broccoli and cucumber.

4 Repeat this process to make a few layers of vegetables and miso, filling up the container. Cover with the lid and leave in the refrigerator for 1–5 days.

5 Take out the vegetables, wash off the miso under running water, then wipe with kitchen paper. Cut the broccoli stem pieces in half then slice into thin strips lengthways. Cut the cucumber into 5mm/¼in thick half-moon slices. Serve cold.

Variation
Carrot, turnip, kohlrabi, celery, radish or thinly sliced cabbage stems can be used in this way.

Pickled broccoli & cucumber: Energy 54kcal/227kJ; Protein 5.6g; Carbohydrate 4.9g, of which sugars 3.8g; Fat 1g, of which saturates 0.2g; Cholesterol 0mg; Calcium 66mg; Fibre 2.9g; Sodium 1789mg.
Lotus stem salad: Energy 43Kcal/181kJ; Protein 1g Carbohydrate 9g, of which sugars 6g; Fat 0g, of which saturates 0g; Cholesterol 0mg; Calcium 0mg; Fibre 0.5mg; Sodium 0.3g

Pepper & Cucumber Salad

Generous quantities of fresh herbs transform familiar ingredients into a wonderful, fresh-tasting side salad.

Serves 4

1 yellow or red (bell) pepper
1 large cucumber
4–5 tomatoes
1 bunch spring onions (scallions)
30ml/2 tbsp fresh parsley
30ml/2 tbsp fresh mint
30ml/2 tbsp fresh
   coriander (cilantro)
2 pitta breads, to serve

For the dressing

2 garlic cloves, crushed
75ml/5 tbsp olive oil
juice of 2 lemons
salt and ground black pepper

1 Halve, seed and core the pepper, then slice. Roughly chop the cucumber and tomatoes. Place in a large salad bowl.

2 Trim and slice the spring onions. Add to the cucumber, tomatoes and pepper. Finely chop the parsley, mint and coriander and add to the bowl. If you have plenty of herbs, you can add as much as you like.

3 To make the dressing, blend the garlic with the olive oil and lemon juice in a bowl, then season to taste with salt and pepper. Pour the dressing over the salad and toss lightly to mix.

4 Toast the pitta breads in a toaster or under a hot grill (broiler) until crisp and serve alongside the salad.

Roasted Red Peppers with Feta, Capers & Preserved Lemons

A delightful burst of piquant fruit gives these sumptuous roast peppers a typically Moroccan flavour. Capers and feta cheese give added flavour to a dish that is quite delicious with kebabs and barbecued meats, as well as with mezze dishes.

Serves 4

4 fleshy, red (bell) peppers
200g/7oz feta cheese, crumbled
30–45ml/2–3 tbsp olive oil or
   argan oil
30ml/2 tbsp capers
peel of 1 preserved lemon, cut
   into small pieces
salt

1 Put the peppers under a hot grill (broiler) and grill (broil) for about 10 minutes, turning frequently, until until the skins have blistered and charred.

2 Transfer the peppers to a bowl, cover with crumpled kitchen paper and leave to cool slightly. Strip off the pepper skins, then remove the stalks and seeds. Slice the flesh and arrange on a serving plate.

3 Add the crumbled feta and pour over the olive or argan oil. Scatter the capers and preserved lemon over the top and sprinkle with a little salt, if required, and serve.

Cook's Tips
• To make preserved lemons, scrub and quarter lemons almost through to the base, then rub the cut sides with salt. Pack tightly into a large sterilized jar. Half fill the jar with more salt, adding some bay leaves, peppercorns and cinnamon, if you like. Cover completely with lemon juice. Cover with a lid and store for 2 weeks, shaking the jar daily. Add a little olive oil to seal and use within 1–6 months, washing off the salt before use.
• Instead of grilling the peppers, you can roast them in a hot oven. Alternatively, thread them onto metal skewers and hold over a gas flame, turning constantly, until charred.

Pepper & cucumber salad: Energy 159kcal/656kJ; Protein 1.8g; Carbohydrate 5.8g, of which sugars 5.6g; Fat 14.4g, of which saturates 2.1g; Cholesterol 0mg; Calcium 46mg; Fibre 2.4g; Sodium 13mg
Red peppers with feta: Energy 223kcal/923kJ; Protein 9.3g; Carbohydrate 10.4g, of which sugars 9.9g; Fat 16.2g, of which saturates 7.8g; Cholesterol 35mg; Calcium 192mg; Fibre 2.4g; Sodium 726mg

Leek & Egg Salad

Smooth-textured leeks are especially delicious warm when partnered with an earthy-rich sauce of parsley, olive oil and walnuts. Serve as a side salad with plainly-grilled or poached fish and new potatoes.

Serves 4
675g/1½lb young leeks
1 egg
fresh parsley sprigs, to garnish

For the dressing
25g/1oz fresh parsley
30ml/2 tbsp olive oil
juice of ½ lemon
50g/2oz/½ cup shelled, broken
    walnuts, toasted
5ml/1 tsp caster (superfine) sugar
salt and ground black pepper

1 Bring a pan of salted water to the boil. Cut the leeks into 10cm/4in lengths and rinse well to flush out any grit or soil. Cook the leeks for 8 minutes. Drain and part-cool under running water.

2 Lower the egg into boiling water and cook for 12 minutes. Cool under cold running water, shell and set aside.

3 To make the dressing, finely chop the parsley in a food processor. Add the olive oil, lemon juice and toasted walnuts. Blend for 1–2 minutes, until smooth.

4 Adjust the consistency with about 90 ml/6 tbsp water. Add the sugar and season to taste with salt and pepper.

5 Place the leeks on an serving plate, then spoon on the sauce. Finely grate (shred) the hard-boiled egg and scatter over the sauce. Garnish with the fresh parsley sprigs and serve while the leeks are still warm.

Cook's Tip
Toast walnuts in a dry non-stick pan (skillet).

Sautéed Herb Salad with Chilli & Preserved Lemon

Firm-leafed fresh herbs, such as flat leaf parsley and mint tossed in a little olive oil and seasoned with salt, are fabulous to serve as a salad in a mezze spread or go wonderfully with spicy kebabs or tagines. Lightly sautéed with garlic and served warm with yogurt, this dish is delightful even on its own.

Serves 4
1 large bunch flat leaf parsley
1 large bunch fresh mint
1 large bunch fresh coriander
    (cilantro)
1 bunch rocket (arugula)
1 large bunch spinach leaves
    (about 115g/4oz)
60–75ml/4–5 tbsp olive oil
2 garlic cloves, finely chopped
1 green or red chilli, seeded
    and finely chopped
½ preserved lemon,
    finely chopped
salt and ground black pepper
45–60ml/3–4 tbsp Greek (US
    strained plain) yogurt, to serve

1 Roughly chop the herbs, rocket and spinach. Set aside.

2 Heat the olive oil in a wide, heavy pan. Stir in the garlic and chilli and fry until they begin to colour.

3 Toss in the herbs, rocket and spinach and cook gently, until they begin to soften and wilt.

4 Add the preserved lemon and season with salt and black pepper to taste.

5 Transfer the salad to a serving dish and serve warm with a dollop of yogurt.

Cook's Tip
This is also good topped with garlic-flavoured yogurt. Simply stir a crushed garlic clove into the yogurt and season to taste.

Leek & egg salad: Energy 197kcal/817kJ; Protein 6.3g; Carbohydrate 6.5g, of which sugars 5.2g; Fat 16.4g, of which saturates 2.1g; Cholesterol 48mg; Calcium 73mg; Fibre 4.5g; Sodium 24mg
Sautéed herb salad: Energy 157kcal/647kJ; Protein 2.9g; Carbohydrate 1.6g, of which sugars 1.5g; Fat 15.6g, of which saturates 2.6g; Cholesterol 0mg; Calcium 135mg; Fibre 2.1g; Sodium 70mg

Braised Artichokes with Fresh Peas

Simple Cooked Salad

This artichoke dish has a unique delicacy. Shelling fresh peas is a little time-consuming but their matchless flavour makes the task very worthwhile. Sit on a step outside in the sunshine, and what at first seems a chore will be positively therapeutic.

Serves 4

4 globe artichokes

juice of 1½ lemons

150ml/¼ pint/⅔ cup extra-virgin olive oil

1 onion, thinly sliced

4–5 spring onions (scallions), roughly chopped

2 carrots, sliced in rounds

1.2kg/2½lb fresh peas in pods, shelled (this will give you about 500–675g/1¼–1½lb peas)

450ml/¾ pint/scant 2 cups hot water

60ml/4 tbsp finely chopped fresh dill

salt and ground black pepper

1 To prepare the artichokes, trim the stalks of the artichokes close to the base, cut the very tips off the leaves and then divide them into quarters. Remove the inedible hairy choke (the central part), carefully scraping the hairs away from the heart at the base of the artichoke. Drop them into a bowl of water acidulated with about one-third of the lemon juice.

2 Heat the olive oil in a wide, shallow pan and add the onion and spring onions, and then a minute later, add the carrots. Sauté the mixture, stirring constantly, for a few seconds, then add the peas and stir for 1–2 minutes to coat them in the oil.

3 Pour in the remaining lemon juice. Let it bubble and evaporate for a few seconds, then add the hot water and bring to the boil. Drain the artichokes and add them to the pan, with salt and pepper to taste. Cover and cook gently for about 40–45 minutes, stirring occasionally.

4 Add the dill and cook for a further 5 minutes, or until the vegetables are tender. Serve hot or at room temperature.

This version of a popular Mediterranean recipe is a versatile side dish.

Serves 4

2 well-flavoured tomatoes, quartered

2 onions, chopped

½ cucumber, halved lengthwise, seeded and sliced

1 green (bell) pepper, halved, seeded and chopped

60ml/4 tbsp water

For the dressing

30ml/2 tbsp lemon juice

45ml/3 tbsp olive oil

2 garlic cloves, crushed

30ml/2 tbsp chopped fresh coriander (cilantro)

salt and ground black pepper

1 Put the prepared tomatoes, onions, cucumber and green pepper into a large pan. Add the water and simmer for 5 minutes. Leave to cool.

2 To make the dressing, whisk together the lemon juice, olive oil and garlic in a bowl.

3 Drain the vegetables, then transfer to a serving bowl. Pour the dressing over the salad, season with salt and pepper to taste and stir in the chopped coriander. Garnish with coriander sprigs and serve immediately.

Braised artichokes with fresh peas: Energy 363kcal/1499kJ; Protein 10.3g; Carbohydrate 20.1g, of which sugars 8.3g; Fat 27.5g, of which saturates 4g; Cholesterol 0mg; Calcium 121mg; Fibre 9.2g; Sodium 91mg

Simple cooked salad: Energy 131kcal/540kJ; Protein 2.2g; Carbohydrate 11g, of which sugars 9.1g; Fat 8.9g, of which saturates 1.3g; Cholesterol 0mg; Calcium 55mg; Fibre 3g; Sodium 14mg

Radicchio, Artichoke & Walnut Salad

The distinctive, earthy taste of Jerusalem artichokes makes a lovely contrast to the sharp freshness of radicchio and lemon. Serve warm or cold as an accompaniment to grilled steak or meats.

Serves 4

1 large radicchio or 150g/5oz radicchio leaves
40g/1½oz/⅓ cup walnut pieces
45ml/3 tbsp walnut oil
thinly pared rind and juice of 1 lemon
500g/1¼lb Jerusalem artichokes
coarse sea salt and ground black pepper
fresh flat leaf parsley, to garnish

1 If using a whole radicchio, cut it into 8–10 wedges. Put the wedges or leaves in a flameproof dish. Scatter over the walnuts, then spoon over the walnut oil and season with salt and pepper. Grill (broil) for 2–3 minutes.

2 Fill a pan with cold water and add half the lemon juice. Using a small, sharp knife, peel the artichokes and cut up any large ones so that the pieces are all roughly the same size. Add them to the pan of acidulated water as you work.

3 Add a pinch of salt to the pan of artichokes, then bring to the boil and cook for 5–7 minutes until tender. Drain. Preheat the grill (broiler) to high.

4 Toss the artichokes into the salad with the remaining lemon juice and the pared rind. Season with coarse salt and pepper.

5 Grill until beginning to brown. Serve garnished with roughly torn parsley.

Spinach & Roast Garlic Salad

Don't worry about the amount of garlic in this salad. During roasting, the garlic becomes sweet and subtle and loses its strong, pungent taste.

Serves 4

12 garlic cloves, unpeeled
60ml/4 tbsp extra-virgin olive oil
450g/1lb baby spinach leaves
50g/2oz/½ cup pine nuts, lightly toasted
juice of ½ lemon
salt and ground black pepper

1 Preheat the oven to 190°C/375°F/Gas 5. Place the garlic in a small roasting pan, toss in 30ml/2 tbsp of the olive oil and roast for about 15 minutes, until the garlic cloves are slightly charred around the edges.

2 While still warm, transfer the garlic to a salad bowl. Add the spinach, pine nuts, lemon juice, remaining olive oil and a little salt. Toss well and add black pepper to taste.

3 Serve immediately, inviting guests to squeeze the softened garlic purée out of the skin to eat.

Radicchio & Chicory Gratin

Creamy béchamel sauce, with its delicate flavour, is the perfect foil for these bitter-tasting salad leaves. Serve with grilled meat for a satisfying meal.

Serves 4

2 heads radicchio, quartered lengthwise
2 heads chicory (Belgian endive), quartered lengthwise
25g/1oz/½ cup drained sun-dried tomatoes in oil, coarsely chopped
25g/1oz/2 tbsp butter
15g/½oz/2 tbsp plain (all-purpose) flour
250ml/8fl oz/1 cup milk
pinch of freshly grated nutmeg
50g/2oz/½ cup grated Emmenthal cheese
salt and ground black pepper
chopped fresh parsley, to garnish

1 Preheat the oven to 180°C/350°F/Gas 4. Grease a 1.2 litre/2 pint/5 cup ovenproof dish and arrange the quartered radicchio and chicory in it.

2 Sprinkle over the sun-dried tomatoes and brush the vegetables with oil from the jar. Sprinkle with salt and pepper and cover the dish with foil. Bake for 15 minutes, then remove the foil and bake for a further 10 minutes.

3 To make the sauce, melt the butter in a small pan, stir in the flour and cook for 1 minute, stirring. Remove from the heat and gradually add the milk, whisking all the time. Return to the heat and bring to the boil, then simmer for about 3 minutes, stirring, to thicken. Season to taste and add the nutmeg.

4 Pour the sauce over the vegetables and sprinkle with the cheese. Bake for 20 minutes until golden.

5 Remove from the oven and serve at once, garnished with parsley if you wish.

Radicchio, artichoke & walnut salad: Energy 179kcal/739kJ; Protein 2.7g; Carbohydrate 7.3g, of which sugars 7.1g; Fat 15.7g, of which saturates 1.4g; Cholesterol 0mg; Calcium 87mg; Fibre 3.1g; Sodium 21mg
Spinach & roast garlic salad: Energy 234kcal/966kJ; Protein 6.1g; Carbohydrate 6g, of which sugars 3.7g; Fat 20.8g, of which saturates 2.3g; Cholesterol 0mg; Calcium 240mg; Fibre 4.6g; Sodium 23mg
Radicchio & chicory gratin: Energy 175kcal/728kJ; Protein 6.9g; Carbohydrate 9g, of which sugars 5.1g; Fat 12.9g, of which saturates 6.5g; Cholesterol 26mg; Calcium 219mg; Fibre 1.5g; Sodium 193mg

Winter Vegetable Salad

This simple side salad is made with leeks, cauliflower and celery, flavoured with wine, herbs and juniper.

Serves 4
450g/1lb leeks
175ml/6fl oz/³⁄₄ cup white wine
5ml/1 tsp olive oil
30ml/2 tbsp lemon juice

2 bay leaves
1 fresh thyme sprig
4 juniper berries
1 small cauliflower, broken into florets
4 celery sticks, sliced on the diagonal
30ml/2 tbsp chopped fresh parsley
salt and ground black pepper

1 Trim the thick green leaves from the leeks and trim off the roots. Rinse well and cut into 2.5cm/1in lengths.

2 Put the wine, olive oil, lemon juice, bay leaves, thyme and juniper berries into a large, heavy-based pan and bring to the boil. Cover and leave to simmer for 20 minutes.

3 Add the leeks, cauliflower and celery. Simmer very gently for 5–6 minutes, or until just tender.

4 Remove the vegetables with a slotted spoon and transfer them to a serving dish. Briskly boil the cooking liquid until reduced by half. Pass through a sieve (strainer).

5 Stir the parsley into the liquid and season with salt and pepper to taste. Pour over the vegetables and leave to cool slightly. Serve at room temperature.

Cook's Tip
Do not overcook the cauliflower; it should have a bit of bite.

Variation
Vary the vegetables for this salad according to the season.

Florets Polonaise

Steamed vegetables make a delicious and extremely healthy accompaniment.

Serves 6
500g/1¼lb cauliflower and broccoli

finely grated rind of ½ lemon
1 large garlic clove, crushed
25g/1oz/½ cup wholegrain breadcrumbs, lightly baked or grilled (broiled) until crisp
2 eggs, hard-boiled and shelled
salt and ground black pepper

1 Trim the cauliflower and broccoli and break into florets, then place in a steamer over a pan of boiling water and steam for about 12 minutes. (If you prefer, boil the vegetables in salted water for 5–7 minutes, until just tender.) Drain the vegetables well and transfer to a warmed serving dish.

2 Meanwhile, make the topping. In a bowl, combine the lemon rind with the garlic and breadcrumbs. Finely chop the eggs and stir into the breadcrumb mixture. Season with salt and black pepper to taste, then sprinkle over the cooked vegetables.

Two Beans Provençal

This would make a tasty side dish for any main course.

Serves 4
5ml/1 tsp olive oil
1 small onion, finely chopped
1 garlic clove, crushed

225g/8oz/scant 1 cup green beans
225g/8oz/scant 1 cup runner (green) beans
2 tomatoes, peeled and chopped
salt and ground black pepper

1 Heat the oil in a heavy or non-stick frying pan, add the onion and sauté over medium heat until softened but not browned.

2 Add the garlic, both beans and the tomatoes. Season well with salt and pepper, then cover tightly. Cook over fairly low heat, shaking the pan from time to time, for about 30 minutes, or until the beans are tender. Serve immediately.

Winter vegetable salad: Energy 110kcal/460kJ; Protein 6.9g; Carbohydrate 8g, of which sugars 6.5g; Fat 2.7g, of which saturates 0.5g; Cholesterol 0mg; Calcium 99mg; Fibre 5.8g; Sodium 44mg
Florets Polonaise: Energy Energy 211kcal/874kJ; Protein 8g; Carbohydrate 5.2g, of which sugars 3.4g; Fat 17.8g, of which saturates 3g; Cholesterol 95mg; Calcium 63mg; Fibre 2.8g; Sodium 51mg
Two beans: Energy 47kcal/195kJ; Protein 2.5g; Carbohydrate 6.3g, of which sugars 5.3g; Fat 1.4g, of which saturates 0.3g; Cholesterol 0mg; Calcium 46mg; Fibre 3.1g; Sodium 5mg

Marinated Mushrooms

This Spanish dish may be served warm or chilled, depending on what you are serving it with. It should be made a day in advance.

Serves 4
30ml/2 tbsp extra virgin olive oil
1 small onion, very finely chopped
1 garlic clove, finely chopped

15ml/1 tbsp tomato purée (paste)
50ml/2fl oz/¼ cup
    amontillado sherry
50ml/2fl oz/¼ cup water
2 cloves
225g/8oz/3 cups button (white)
    mushrooms, trimmed
salt and ground black pepper
chopped fresh parsley, to garnish

1 Heat the oil in a pan. Add the onion and garlic and cook until soft. Stir in the tomato purée, sherry, water and the cloves and season with salt and black pepper.

2 Bring to the boil, cover and simmer gently for 45 minutes, adding more water if the mixture becomes too dry.

3 Add the mushrooms to the pan, then cover and allow to simmer for about 5 minutes. Remove from the heat and allow to cool, still covered.

4 Chill the mushrooms in the refrigerator overnight so that they take on the flavours. Either gently heat the mushrooms to serve or eat them chilled, sprinkled with the chopped parsley.

Green Beans with Almond Butter

A perfect accompaniment for baked or grilled oily fish.

Serves 4
350g/12oz green beans, trimmed
50g/2oz/¼ cup butter

50g/2oz/⅓ cup whole blanched
    almonds
grated (shredded) rind and juice
    of 1 unwaxed lemon
salt and ground black pepper

1 Cook the beans in a pan of salted boiling water for about 3 minutes, or until just tender. Drain well. Meanwhile, melt the butter in a large non-stick pan until foamy.

2 Add the almonds to the pan and cook, stirring occasionally, for 2–3 minutes, or until golden. Remove from the heat and toss with the beans, lemon rind and juice, and season.

Chicory Salad with Roquefort

A quick and elegant accompaniment to steak or baked mushrooms, this salad combines creamy, rich cheese with delicious crisp leaves and toasted walnuts.

Serves 4
30ml/2 tbsp red wine vinegar
5ml/1 tsp Dijon mustard

50ml/2oz/1/4 cup wlanut oil
15–30ml/1–2tbsp sunflower oil
2 white or red chicory heads
1 celery heart or 4 celery sticks,
    cut into julienne strips
75g/3oz/3/4 cup walnut halves,
    lightly toasted
115g/4oz Roquefort cheese
salt and ground black pepper
fresh parsley sprigs, to garnish

1 Whisk together the vinegar, mustard and salt and pepper to taste in a small bowl. Slowly whisk in the oils to make a vinaigrette.

2 Arrange the chicory on individual serving plates. Scatter over the celery and toasted walnut halves. Crumble the Roquefort cheese on top of each salad and grill for 1 minute to just soften the cheese and colour the leaf edges a little. Drizzle over a little vinaigrette and garnish with parsley sprigs.

Marinated mushrooms: Energy 80kcal/329kJ; Protein 1.4g; Carbohydrate 2.1g, of which sugars 1.7g; Fat 5.8g, of which saturates 0.9g; Cholesterol 0mg; Calcium 9mg; Fibre 0.9g; Sodium 14mg
Green beans with almond butter: Energy 191kcal/786kJ; Protein 4.4g; Carbohydrate 3.7g, of which sugars 2.6g; Fat 17.7g, of which saturates 7.2g; Cholesterol 27mg; Calcium 64mg; Fibre 2.9g; Sodium 78mg
Chicory Salad with Roquefort: Energy 361kcal/1488kJ; Protein 9.4g; Carbohydrate 1.5g, of which sugars 1.3g; Fat 35.3g, of which saturates 7.9g; Cholesterol 22mg; Calcium 204mg; Fibre 1.8g; Sodium 423mg

French Bean Salad

Green beans are delicious served with a simple vinaigrette dressing, but this slightly more elaborate dish turns them into something quite special.

Serves 4
450g/1lb green beans
15ml/1 tbsp olive oil
25g/1oz butter
½ garlic clove, crushed
50g/2oz/1 cup fresh white
   breadcrumbs
15ml/1 tbsp chopped
   fresh parsley
1 hard-boiled (hard-cooked) egg,
   finely chopped

For the dressing
30ml/2 tbsp olive oil
30ml/2 tbsp sunflower oil
10ml/2 tsp white wine vinegar
½ garlic clove, crushed
1.5ml/¼ tsp Dijon mustard
pinch of sugar
pinch of salt

1 Cook the green beans in boiling salted water for 5–6 minutes, until tender. Drain, refresh under cold running water and place in a serving bowl.

2 To make the dressing, mix all the ingredients thoroughly together. Pour over the beans and toss.

3 Heat the oil and butter in a non-stick pan and fry the garlic for 1 minute. Stir in the breadcrumbs and fry over a medium heat for about 3–4 minutes, until golden brown, stirring frequently.

4 Remove the pan from the heat and stir in the parsley and then the egg. Sprinkle the breadcrumb mixture over the green beans. Serve warm or at room temperature.

> **Variation**
> For a mixed bean salad, cook the green beans and dressing as above, then put the beans in a salad bowl with two finely chopped celery sticks, a few finely chopped spring onions (scallions), chopped parsley and a drained and rinsed can of red kidney beans or mixed beans. Toss in the dressing.

Spicy Sweetcorn Salad

This brilliant, sweet-tasting salad is served warm with a spicy dressing. It goes extremely well with grilled pork or steaks.

Serves 4
30ml/2 tbsp vegetable oil
450g/1lb canned corn
1 green (bell) pepper, seeded
   and diced
1 small red chilli, seeded
   and diced
4 spring onions (scallions), sliced
45ml/3 tbsp chopped parsley
225g/8oz cherry tomatoes, halved
salt and ground black pepper

For the dressing
2.5ml/½ tsp sugar
30ml/2 tbsp white wine vinegar
2.5ml/½ tsp Dijon mustard
15ml/1 tbsp chopped fresh basil
15ml/1 tbsp mayonnaise
1.5ml/¼ tsp chilli sauce

1 Cook the drained corn, pepper, chilli and spring onions in the oil for 5 minutes, stirring, until softened. Transfer to a salad bowl. Stir in the parsley and the cherry tomatoes.

2 To make the dressing, whisk all the ingredients together. Pour over the corn mixture. Season with salt and pepper. Toss well to combine, then serve while the salad is still warm.

French bean salad: Energy 260kcal/1076kJ; Protein 5.2g; Carbohydrate 13.3g, of which sugars 3g; Fat 21.1g, of which saturates 5.6g; Cholesterol 61mg; Calcium 65mg; Fibre 2.8g; Sodium 151mg
Spicy sweetcorn salad: Energy 205kcal/863kJ; Protein 4.3g; Carbohydrate 32.5g, of which sugars 15.3g; Fat 7.3g, of which saturates 1.1g; Cholesterol 3mg; Calcium 39mg; Fibre 3.4g; Sodium 298mg

Beetroot & Potato Salad

A brightly coloured salad with a lovely texture. The sweetness of the beetroot contrasts perfectly with the tangy dressing. Ideal with a selection of cold meats.

Serves 4

4 medium beetroot (beet)
4 potatoes, peeled and diced
I red onion, finely chopped
150ml/¼ pint/⅔ cup natural (plain) yogurt
10ml/2 tsp cider vinegar
2 small sweet and sour cucumbers, finely chopped
10ml/2 tsp creamed horseradish
salt and ground black pepper
parsley sprigs, to garnish

I Trim the leafy stalks of the beetroot down to about 2.5cm/1in of the root. Wash the beetroot but do not peel. Boil the unpeeled beetroot in a large pan of water for 40 minutes or until tender.

2 Meanwhile, boil the diced potatoes in a separate pan for 20 minutes until just tender.

3 When the beetroot are cooked, rinse and remove the skins. Chop into rough pieces and place in a bowl. Drain the potatoes and add to the bowl, together with the onions.

4 Mix the yogurt, vinegar, cucumbers and horseradish. Reserve a little for a garnish and pour the remainder over the salad. Toss and serve with parsley sprigs and remaining dressing.

Cook's Tip
If you are short of time, buy vacuum-packed ready-cooked and peeled beetroot, available in most supermarkets.

Variation
Add toasted chopped hazelnuts to the yogurt dressing.

Asparagus with Egg & Lemon Sauce

Eggs and lemons are often found in dishes from Greece, Turkey and the Middle East. This sauce has a tangy, fresh taste and brings out the best in asparagus.

Serves 4

675g/1½lb asparagus, woody ends removed, and tied into a bundle
15ml/1 tbsp cornflour (cornstarch)
10ml/2 tsp sugar
2 egg yolks
juice of 1½ lemons
salt

I Cook the bundle of asparagus in boiling salted water for 7–10 minutes until just tender.

2 Drain well, reserving 200ml/7fl oz/scant 1 cup of the cooking liquid. Arrange the asparagus spears in a serving dish.

3 Blend the cornflour with the cooled, reserved cooking liquid in a small pan. Bring to the boil, stirring constantly, and cook over a gentle heat until the sauce thickens slightly. Stir in the sugar, then remove from the heat and allow to cool slightly.

4 Beat the egg yolks thoroughly with the lemon juice and gradually stir into the cooled sauce. Cook over a very low heat, stirring all the time, until the sauce is fairly thick. Be careful not to overheat the sauce or it may curdle. As soon as the sauce has thickened, remove the pan from the heat and continue stirring for 1 minute. Taste and add salt or sugar as necessary. Allow the sauce to cool slightly.

5 Stir the cooled sauce, then pour a little over the asparagus. Serve warm with the rest of the sauce.

Variation
This dish is also delicious served cold: chill for at least 2 hours.

Beetroot & potato salad: Energy 141kcal/597kJ; Protein 5.8g; Carbohydrate 28.8g, of which sugars 12.9g; Fat 1.2g, of which saturates 0.3g; Cholesterol 1mg; Calcium 107mg; Fibre 3.4g; Sodium 144mg
Asparagus with egg & lemon sauce: Energy 96kcal/399kJ; Protein 6.4g; Carbohydrate 9.5g, of which sugars 5.8g; Fat 3.8g, of which saturates 1g; Cholesterol 101mg; Calcium 59mg; Fibre 2.9g; Sodium 8mg

Globe Artichokes with Beans & Aioli

Make the most of fresh artichokes when in season by serving them with a squeeze of lemon and this delicious Spanish garlic and mayonnaise dressing.

Serves 3
225g/8oz green beans
3 small globe artichokes

15ml/1 tbsp olive oil
pared rind of 1 lemon
coarse salt, for sprinkling
lemon wedges, to garnish

For the aioli
6 large garlic cloves, thinly sliced
10ml/2 tsp white wine vinegar
250ml/8fl oz/1 cup olive oil
salt and ground black pepper

1 To make the aioli, put the garlic and vinegar in a food processor or blender. With the motor running, slowly pour in the olive oil through the lid or feeder tube until the mixture is quite thick and smooth. Season with salt and pepper to taste.

2 To make the salad, cook the green beans in lightly salted boiling water for 1–2 minutes until slightly softened. Drain well.

3 Trim the artichoke stalks close to the base. Cook the artichokes in a large pan of salted water for about 30 minutes, or until you can easily pull away a leaf from the base. Drain. Cut the artichokes in half lengthwise and carefully scrape out the hairy choke using a teaspoon.

4 Arrange the artichokes and beans on serving plates and drizzle with the olive oil. Sprinkle the lemon rind over them and season to taste with coarse salt and a little pepper. Spoon the aïoli into the artichoke hearts and serve the salad warm, garnished with lemon wedges.

5 To eat the artichokes, squeeze a little lemon juice over them, then pull the leaves from the base one at a time and use to scoop a little of the aïoli sauce. Gently scrape away the white, fleshy end of each leaf with your teeth and discard the rest of the leaf. Eat the base of the artichoke with a knife and fork.

Grilled Fennel Salad

This is so typically Italian that if you close your eyes you could be on a Tuscan hillside, enjoying an elegant lunch. Fennel has many fans, but is often used only in its raw state or lightly braised, making this griddle recipe a delightful discovery.

Serves 6
3 sweet baby orange (bell) peppers

5 fennel bulbs with green tops, about 900g/2lb total weight
30ml/2 tbsp olive oil
15ml/1 tbsp cider or white wine vinegar
45ml/3 tbsp extra-virgin olive oil
24 small niçoise olives
2 long sprigs of fresh savory, leaves removed
salt and ground black pepper

1 Heat a griddle until a few drops of water sprinkled onto the surface evaporate instantly. Roast the baby peppers, turning them every few minutes until charred all over. Remove the pan from the heat, place the peppers in a bowl and cover with clear film (plastic wrap).

2 Remove the green fronds from the fennel and reserve. Slice the fennel lengthwise into five roughly equal pieces. If the root looks a little tough, cut it out. Place the fennel pieces in a flat dish, coat with the olive oil and season with salt and pepper. Rub off the charred skin from the grilled peppers, remove the seeds and cut the flesh into small dice.

3 Re-heat the griddle and test the temperature again, then lower the heat slightly and grill the fennel slices in batches for about 8–10 minutes, turning frequently, until they are branded with golden grill marks. Monitor the heat so they cook through without over charring. As each batch cooks, transfer it to a flat serving dish.

4 Whisk the vinegar and extra-virgin olive oil together, then pour over the fennel. Gently fold in the diced baby orange peppers and the niçoise olives. Tear the savory leaves and fennel fronds and scatter over the salad. Serve warm.

Globe artichokes with beans & aioli: Energy 540kcal/2221kJ; Protein 2.1g; Carbohydrate 3.6g, of which sugars 2.9g; Fat 57.6g, of which saturates 8.2g; Cholesterol 0mg; Calcium 82mg; Fibre 3.1g; Sodium 80mg
Grilled fennel salad: Energy 139kcal/574kJ; Protein 2.4g; Carbohydrate 8.7g, of which sugars 8.3g; Fat 10.8g, of which saturates 1.6g; Cholesterol 0mg; Calcium 49mg; Fibre 5.3g; Sodium 208mg

Roasted Beetroot with Horseradish

Fresh beetroot is enjoying a well-deserved renaissance. It is very nutritious, full-flavoured and versatile. Roasting gives it a delicious sweet flavour, which contrasts wonderfully with this sharp, tangy dressing.

Serves 4
450g/1lb baby beetroot (beet), preferably with leaves
15ml/1 tbsp olive oil

For the dressing
30ml/2 tbsp lemon juice
30ml/2 tbsp mirin or saké
120ml/8 tbsp olive oil
30ml/2 tbsp creamed horseradish
salt and ground black pepper

1 Cook the unpeeled beetroot in boiling salted water for 30 minutes. Drain, add the olive oil and toss gently. Preheat the oven to 200°C/400°F/Gas 6.

2 Place the beetroot on a baking sheet and roast for about 40 minutes or until tender when pierced with a knife.

3 Meanwhile, make the dressing. Whisk together the lemon juice, mirin or saké, olive oil and horseradish until smooth and creamy. Season with salt and pepper to taste.

4 Peel the beetroot, cut it in half, place in a bowl and add the dressing. Toss gently and serve immediately.

Cook's Tips
• This salad is probably at its best served warm, but you can make it in advance, if you wish, and serve it at room temperature. Add the dressing just before serving.
• Beetroot has a reputation for containing cancer-fighting compounds and is thought to enhance the immune system. It is a powerful blood-purifier and is rich in iron, vitamins C and A, and folates, which are essential for healthy cells.

Young Vegetables with Tarragon

The vegetables for this bright, fresh dish are just lightly cooked to bring out their different flavours. The tarragon adds a wonderful depth to the salad. Try serving as a light side dish with fish and seafood dishes.

Serves 4
5 spring onions (scallions)

50g/2oz/¼ cup butter
1 garlic clove, crushed
115g/4oz asparagus tips
115g/4oz mangetouts (snow peas), trimmed
115g/4oz broad (fava) beans
2 Little Gem (Bibb) lettuces
5ml/1 tsp finely chopped fresh tarragon
salt and ground black pepper

1 Cut the spring onions into quarters lengthwise and fry gently over a medium-low heat in half the butter with the garlic.

2 Add the asparagus tips, mangetouts and broad beans. Mix well to coat all the pieces with oil.

3 Add enough water to just cover the base of the pan, then season with salt and pepper to taste. Bring to the boil, then allow to simmer gently for a few minutes.

4 Cut the lettuce into quarters and add to the pan. Cook for 3 minutes, then remove from the heat, swirl in the remaining butter and the tarragon, season and serve.

Roasted beetroot with horseradish: Energy 254kcal/1052kJ; Protein 2.1g; Carbohydrate 10g, of which sugars 9.1g; Fat 22.2g, of which saturates 3.2g; Cholesterol 1mg; Calcium 26mg; Fibre 2.3g; Sodium 143mg
Young vegetables with tarragon: Energy 149Kcal/619kJ; Protein 4.7g; Carbohydrate 6.1g, of which sugars 3g; Fat 12g, of which saturates 7.3g; Cholesterol 29mg; calcium 55mg; Fibre 3.5g; Sodium 89mg

Thai Cabbage Salad

This is a simple and delicious way of serving a somewhat mundane vegetable. Classic Thai flavours permeate this colourful warm salad.

Serves 4–6
30ml/2 tbsp vegetable oil
2 large fresh red chillies, seeded and cut into thin strips

6 garlic cloves, thinly sliced
6 shallots, thinly sliced
1 small cabbage, shredded
30ml/2 tbsp coarsely chopped roasted peanuts, to garnish

For the dressing
30ml/2 tbsp Thai fish sauce
grated (shredded) rind of 1 lime
30ml/2 tbsp fresh lime juice
120ml/4fl oz/½ cup coconut milk

1 To make the dressing, mix the fish sauce, lime rind and juice and coconut milk in a bowl. Whisk until thoroughly combined and set aside.

2 Heat the oil in a wok. Stir-fry the chillies, garlic and shallots over a medium heat for 3–4 minutes, until the shallots are brown and crisp. Remove with a slotted spoon and set aside.

3 Bring a large pan of lightly salted water to the boil. Add the cabbage and blanch for 2–3 minutes. Turn into a colander, drain well and transfer to a bowl.

4 Whisk the dressing again, add it to the warm cabbage and toss to mix. Transfer the salad to a serving dish. Sprinkle with the fried shallot mixture and the peanuts. Serve immediately.

> **Cook's Tip**
> Buy coconut milk in cans from supermarkets and ethnic stores.

> **Variation**
> Other vegetables, such as cauliflower, broccoli and Chinese leaves (Chinese cabbage), can be cooked in this way.

Stir-fried Pineapple, Ginger & Chilli

Throughout South-east Asia, fruit is often treated like a vegetable and tossed in a salad, or stir-fried, to accompany spicy dishes.

Serves 4
30ml/2 tbsp groundnut (peanut) oil
2 garlic cloves, finely shredded
40g/1½oz fresh root ginger, peeled and finely shredded
2 red Thai chillies, seeded and finely shredded

1 pineapple, trimmed, peeled, cored and cut into bitesize chunks
15ml/1 tbsp Thai fish sauce
30ml/2 tbsp soy sauce
15ml–30ml/1–2 tbsp sugar
30ml/2 tbsp roasted unsalted peanuts, finely chopped
1 lime, cut into quarters, to serve

1 Heat a large wok or heavy pan and add the oil. Stir in the garlic, ginger and chilli. Stir-fry until they begin to colour.

2 Add the pineapple and stir-fry until the edges turn golden.

3 Stir in the fish sauce, soy sauce and sugar to taste and continue to stir-fry until the pineapple begins to caramelize.

4 Transfer the salad to a serving dish, sprinkle with the roasted peanuts and serve with lime wedges.

Thai cabbage salad: Energy 798kcal/3334kJ; Protein 38.5g; Carbohydrate 131.8g, of which sugars 127.7g; Fat 14.3g, of which saturates 1.4g; Cholesterol 0mg; Calcium 1259mg; Fibre 53.7g; Sodium 461mg
Stir-fried pineapple: Energy 203kcal/844kJ; Protein 2.7g; Carbohydrate 16g, of which sugars 15.4g; Fat 14.7g, of which saturates 1.9g; Cholesterol 0mg; Calcium 31mg; Fibre 1.8g; Sodium 810mg

Stewed Aubergine

Stewing aubergines with tomatoes, red wine and garlic really brings out the best in this delectable Mediterranean vegetable.

Serves 4

1 large aubergine (eggplant)
60–90ml/4–6 tbsp olive oil
2 shallots, thinly sliced
4 tomatoes, quartered
2 garlic cloves, thinly sliced
60ml/4 tbsp red wine
30ml/2 tbsp chopped fresh
 parsley, plus extra to garnish
30–45ml/2–3 tbsp virgin olive oil
 (if serving cold)
salt and ground black pepper

1 Slice the aubergine into 1cm/½in rounds. Layer the aubergine slices in a colander, sprinkling each layer with a little salt. Leave to drain over a sink or plate for about 20 minutes.

2 Rinse the aubergine slices well, then press between several layers of kitchen paper to remove any excess liquid.

3 Heat 30ml/2 tbsp of the oil in a large frying pan (skillet) until smoking. Add one layer of aubergine slices and fry, turning once, until golden brown. Transfer to a plate covered with kitchen paper. Heat more oil and fry the second batch in the same way.

4 Heat 15ml/1 tbsp of oil in a pan and cook the shallots for 5 minutes until golden. Cut the aubergine into strips and add to the shallots with the tomatoes, garlic and wine. Cover and simmer for 30 minutes.

5 Stir in the parsley, and check the seasonings. Sprinkle with a little more parsley and serve hot. To serve cold, dribble a little virgin olive oil over the dish before it goes on the table.

> **Cook's Tip**
> Heat the oil before adding the aubergine (eggplant) slices and do not be tempted to add more oil once the aubergines are cooking as they will absorb cold oil, resulting in a greasy dish.

Roast Mediterranean Vegetables with Pecorino

Aubergines, courgettes, peppers and tomatoes make a marvellous medley when roasted and served drizzled with fragrant olive oil. Shavings of sheep's milk Pecorino add the perfect finishing touch.

Serves 4-6

1 aubergine (eggplant), sliced
2 courgettes (zucchini), sliced
2 red or yellow (bell) peppers,
 seeded and quartered
1 large onion, thickly sliced
2 large carrots, cut into sticks
4 firm plum tomatoes, halved
extra-virgin olive oil, for brushing
 and sprinkling
45ml/3 tbsp chopped
 fresh parsley
45ml/3 tbsp pine nuts,
 lightly toasted
125g/4oz piece of
 Pecorino cheese
salt and ground black pepper

1 Layer the aubergine slices in a colander, sprinkling each layer with a little salt. Leave to drain over a sink or plate for about 20 minutes, then rinse thoroughly under cold running water, drain well and pat dry with kitchen paper. Preheat the oven to 220°C/425°F/Gas 7.

2 Spread out the aubergine slices, courgettes, peppers, onion, carrots and tomatoes in one or two large roasting pans. Brush the vegetables lightly with olive oil and roast them in the oven for about 20 minutes or until they are lightly browned and the skins on the peppers have begun to blister.

3 Transfer the vegetables to a large serving platter. If you like, peel the peppers. Trickle over any vegetable juices from the pan and season to taste with salt and pepper. As the vegetables cool, sprinkle them with more oil (preferably extra-virgin olive oil). When they are at room temperature, mix in the parsley and pine nuts.

4 Using a vegetable peeler, shave the Pecorino and scatter the shavings over the vegetables.

Stewed aubergine: Energy 135kcal/560kJ; Protein 1.4g; Carbohydrate 5.2g, of which sugars 4.7g; Fat 11.6g, of which saturates 1.7g; Cholesterol 0mg; Calcium 17mg; Fibre 2.5g; Sodium 10mg
Roast Mediterranean vegetables: Energy 202kcal/839kJ; Protein 12g; Carbohydrate 10g, of which sugars 9.3g; Fat 12.9g, of which saturates 4.8g; Cholesterol 21mg; Calcium 300mg; Fibre 4g; Sodium 244mg

Lentil Salad with Red Onion & Garlic

This delicious, garlicky lentil salad is perfect served with meaty kebabs. It can be served warm or cooled. As a finishing touch, serve it with a generous spoonful of thick, creamy yogurt.

Serves 4
45ml/3 tbsp olive oil
2 red onions, chopped
2 tomatoes, peeled, seeded and chopped
10ml/2 tsp ground turmeric
10ml/2 tsp ground cumin
175g/6oz/³⁄₄ cup brown or green lentils, picked over and rinsed
900ml/1¹⁄₂ pints/3³⁄₄ cups vegetable stock or water
4 garlic cloves, crushed
1 small bunch fresh coriander (cilantro), finely chopped
salt and ground black pepper
1 lemon, cut into wedges, to serve

1 Heat 30ml/2 tbsp of the oil in a large pan or flameproof casserole and fry the onions until soft.

2 Add the tomatoes, turmeric and cumin, then stir in the lentils. Pour in the stock or water and bring to the boil, then reduce the heat and simmer until the lentils are tender and almost all the liquid has been absorbed.

3 In a separate pan, fry the garlic in the remaining oil until brown and frizzled.

4 Toss the garlic into the lentils with the fresh coriander and season to taste. Serve warm or at room temperature, with wedges of lemon for squeezing over.

> **Cook's Tip**
> If you prefer, you can replace the lentils with mung beans – they work just as well. When including this type of dish in a mezze spread, it is worth balancing it with a dip such as zahdouk and a fruity salad for the different textures.

Grilled Mixed Onion Salad

This salad is brilliant served with grilled meat and fish.

Serves 4
6 red spring onions (scallions), trimmed
6 green salad onions, trimmed and split lengthwise
250g/9oz small or baby (pearl) onions, peeled and left whole
2 pink onions, sliced horizontally into 5mm/4in rounds
2 red onions, sliced
into wedges
2 small yellow onions, sliced into wedges
4 banana shallots, halved lengthwise
200g/7oz shallots
45ml/3 tbsp olive oil, plus extra for drizzling
juice of 1 lemon
45ml/3 tbsp chopped fresh flat leaf parsley
30ml/2 tbsp balsamic vinegar
salt and ground black pepper

1 Preheat the grill. Spread the onions and shallots in a large flat dish. Whisk the oil and lemon juice together and pour over. Turn the onions and shallots in the dressing to coat them evenly. Season to taste.

2 Put the onions and shallots on a griddle or perforated metal vegetable basket placed on the grill rack. Cook for 5–7 minutes, turning occasionally. Alternatively, cook the onions under a conventional grill (broiler).

3 Just before serving, add the parsley and gently toss to mix, then drizzle over the balsamic vinegar and extra olive oil.

Spciy Carrot Salad

Packed with exotic spices, this colourful Middle-Eastern salad is sure to go down well. It is delicious served with a topping of tangy, garlicky yogurt.

Serves 4
450g/1lb carrots, cut into sticks
30–45ml/2–3 tbsp olive oil
juice of 1 lemon
2–3 garlic cloves, crushed
10ml/2 tsp sugar
5–10ml/1–2 tsp cumin
   seeds, roasted
5ml/1 tsp ground cinnamon
5ml/1 tsp paprika
1 small bunch fresh coriander
   (cilantro), finely chopped
1 small bunch fresh mint, finely
   chopped
salt and ground black pepper

1 Steam the carrots over boiling water for about 15 minutes, or until tender.

2 While they are still warm, toss the carrots in a serving bowl with the olive oil, lemon juice, garlic and sugar.

3 Season to taste, then add the cumin seeds, cinnamon and paprika. Finally, toss in the fresh coriander and mint, and serve warm or at room temperature.

Cook's Tip
To roast the cumin seeds, stir them in a heavy pan over a low heat until they change colour slightly and emit a warm, nutty aroma. Be careful not to burn them.

Variation
For a spiced carrot dip, put 3 grated carrots, 1 chopped onion and the grated rind and juice of 2 oranges in a pan with 15ml/1 tbsp hot curry paste. Bring to the boil, then simmer for 10 minutes until tender. Process until smooth, allow to cool. Stir in 150ml/¼ pint/⅔ cup natural (plain) yogurt. Add a handful basil, then season with lemon juice and salt and pepper. Serve.

Moroccan Carrot Salad

A cumin and coriander vinaigrette lifts this carrot salad out of the ordinary. Fresh tasting and lightly spiced, it makes a lovely accompaniment for all sorts of dishes.

Serves 4–6
3–4 carrots
pinch of sugar
3–4 garlic cloves, chopped
1.5ml/¼ tsp ground cumin,
   or to taste
juice of ½ lemon
30–45ml/2–3 tbsp extra-virgin
   olive oil
15–30ml/1–2 tbsp red wine
   vinegar or fruit vinegar, such
   as raspberry
30ml/2 tbsp chopped fresh
   coriander (cilantro) leaves or
   a mixture of coriander
   and parsley
salt and ground black pepper
fresh coriander (cilantro) sprigs,
   to garnish (optional)

1 Thinly slice the carrots. Cook the carrots by either steaming or boiling in lightly salted water until they are just tender but not soft. Drain well, leave for a few moments to dry, then put them in a serving bowl.

2 Add the sugar, chopped garlic, ground cumin, lemon juice, olive oil and red wine vinegar to the carrots and toss them together. Add the chopped herbs and season with salt and pepper to taste. Serve warm, garnished with coriander sprigs, if using.

Spicy carrot salad: Energy 114kcal/473kJ; Protein 1.6g; Carbohydrate 13.2g, of which sugars 11.2g; Fat 6.5g, of which saturates 1g; Cholesterol 0mg; Calcium 61mg; Fibre 3.3g; Sodium 34mg
Moroccan carrot salad: Energy 53kcal/220kJ; Protein 0.6g; Carbohydrate 4.2g, of which sugars 3.9g; Fat 3.9g, of which saturates 0.6g; Cholesterol 0mg; Calcium 29mg; Fibre 1.6g; Sodium 15mg

Lemony Carrots

The carrots are cooked until just tender in a lemony stock which is then thickened to make a light tangy sauce.

Serves 4

450g/1lb carrots, thinly sliced
bouquet garni
15ml/1 tbsp freshly squeezed
   lemon juice
pinch of freshly grated nutmeg
20g/¾ oz/1½ tbsp butter
15ml/½ oz/1 tbsp plain
   (all-purpose) flour
salt and ground black pepper

1 Bring 600ml/1 pint/2½ cups water to the boil in a large pan, then add the carrots, bouquet garni and lemon juice. Add a pinch of nutmeg and season to taste with salt and pepper.

2 Bring back to the boil, then lower the heat slightly and simmer until the carrots are tender. Remove the carrots using a slotted spoon, then keep warm.

3 Boil the cooking liquid hard until it has reduced to about 300ml/½ pint/1¼ cups. Discard the bouquet garni.

4 Mash 15g/½oz/1 tbsp of the butter and all of the flour together, then gradually whisk into the simmering reduced cooking liquid, whisking well after each addition. Continue to simmer for about 3 minutes, stirring frequently, until the sauce has thickened.

5 Return the carrots to the pan, heat through in the sauce, then remove from the heat. Stir in the remaining butter and serve immediately.

Cook's Tip
A bouquet garni is a small bunch of herbs, usually bay leaves, parsley and thyme, tied together with string or in a muslin bag. If you make your own, you can add different herbs to suit a dish. Dried bouquet garnis are sold in supermarkets.

Braised Red Cabbage with Apples

Lightly spiced with a sharp-sweet flavour, this dish goes well with roast pork, duck and game dishes.

Serves 4–6

1kg/2lb red cabbage
2 onions, chopped
2 cooking apples, peeled, cored
   and grated
5ml/1 tsp freshly grated nutmeg
1.5ml/¼ tsp ground cloves
1.5ml/¼ tsp ground cinnamon
15g/½ oz/1 tbsp soft dark brown
   sugar
45ml/3 tbsp red wine vinegar
25g/1oz/2 tbsp butter or
   margarine, diced
salt and ground black pepper

1 Preheat the oven to 160°C/325°F/Gas 3. Cut away and discard the large white ribs from the outer cabbage leaves using a large sharp knife, then finely shred the cabbage.

2 Layer the shredded cabbage in a large ovenproof dish with the onions, apples, spices and sugar, seasoning with salt and pepper. Pour over the red wine vinegar and add the diced butter or margarine.

3 Cover the ovenproof dish and cook in the oven for about 1½ hours, stirring a couple of times, until the cabbage is very tender. Serve immediately.

Cook's Tips
• This recipe can be cooked in advance. Bake the cabbage for 1½ hours, then cool. To complete the cooking, oven bake at the same temperature for about 30 minutes, stirring occasionally.
• Add a splash of red wine if the dish starts to look dry during cooking, then add a little extra sugar to taste.

Variation
Try adding a strip of orange rind to the dish during cooking, then remove before serving.

Lemony carrots: Energy 89kcal/372kJ; Protein 1.1g; Carbohydrate 11.8g, of which sugars 8.4g; Fat 4.5g, of which saturates 2.7g; Cholesterol 11mg; Calcium 34mg; Fibre 2.8g; Sodium 59mg.
Braised cabbage: Energy 121kcal/508kJ; Protein 3.1g; Carbohydrate 19.4g, of which sugars 18.1g; Fat 3.9g, of which saturates 2.2g; Cholesterol 9mg; Calcium 98mg; Fibre 5g; Sodium 40mg

Red Cabbage with Pears & Nuts

A sweet and sour, spicy red cabbage dish, with the added juiciness of pears and extra crunch of walnuts.

Serves 6

15ml/1 tbsp walnut oil
1 onion, sliced
2 whole star anise
5ml/1 tsp ground cinnamon
pinch of ground cloves
450g/1lb red cabbage,
    finely shredded
25g/1oz/2 tbsp soft dark
    brown sugar
45ml/3 tbsp red wine vinegar
300ml/½ pint/1¼ cups red wine
150ml/¼ pint/⅔ cup port
2 pears, cut into 1cm/½in cubes
115g/4oz/⅔ cup raisins
115g/4oz/1 cup walnut halves
salt and ground black pepper

1 Heat the oil in a large heavy pan. Add the sliced onion and cook over low heat, stirring occasionally, for about 5 minutes until softened.

2 Add the star anise, cinnamon, cloves and cabbage and cook for about 3 minutes more.

3 Stir in the sugar, vinegar, red wine and port. Cover the pan and simmer gently for 10 minutes, stirring occasionally.

4 Stir in the cubed pears and raisins and cook without replacing the lid for a further 10 minutes, or until the cabbage is tender. Season to taste with salt and pepper. Mix in the walnut halves and serve immediately.

Cook's Tip
The vinegar and wine help to preserve the beautiful colour of the cabbage as well as adding to the flavour.

Variation
Omit the star anise and cinnamon and add 15ml/1tbsp juniper berries with the ground cloves.

Ratatouille

Bursting with Mediterranean flavours, this tasty dish may be served hot or cold, as a tasty starter, side dish or vegetarian main course.

Serves 4

2 large aubergines (eggplants),
    roughly chopped
150ml/¼ pint/⅔ cup olive oil
2 onions, sliced
2 garlic cloves, chopped
4 courgettes (zucchini), roughly
    chopped
1 large red (bell) pepper, seeded
    and roughly chopped
2 large yellow (bell) peppers,
    seeded and roughly chopped
1 fresh rosemary sprig
1 fresh thyme sprig
5ml/1 tsp coriander seeds,
    crushed
3 plum tomatoes, peeled, seeded
    and chopped
8 basil leaves, roughly torn
salt and ground black pepper
fresh parsley or basil sprigs,
    to garnish

1 Place the aubergines in a colander, sprinkle with salt and place a plate with a weight on top. Leave for 30 minutes to extract the bitter juices.

2 Heat the olive oil in a large pan and gently fry the onions for about 6–7 minutes until just softened. Add the garlic and cook for a further 2 minutes, stirring frequently.

3 Rinse the aubergines under cold running water, then drain and pat dry with kitchen paper. Add the aubergines to the pan of onions, together with the courgettes and peppers. Increase the heat and sauté for a few minutes until just turning brown.

4 Add the rosemary, thyme and coriander seeds, then cover the pan and cook gently for about 30 minutes.

5 Add the tomatoes and season to taste with salt and pepper. Cook gently for a further 10 minutes, until the vegetables are soft but not too mushy.

6 Remove the sprigs of herbs. Stir in the torn basil leaves and adjust the seasoning. Leave to cool slightly and serve warm or cold, garnished with sprigs of parsley or basil.

Cabbage with pears: Energy 202kcal/847kJ; Protein 1.8g; Carbohydrate 30.1g, of which sugars 29.8g; Fat 2.1g, of which saturates 0.2g; Cholesterol 0mg; Calcium 60mg; Fibre 3.2g; Sodium 23mg

Ratatouille: Energy 349kcal/1442kJ; Protein 6.4g; Carbohydrate 21.6g, of which sugars 19.1g; Fat 26.9g, of which saturates 4g; Cholesterol 0mg; Calcium 82mg; Fibre 7.3g; Sodium 18mg

Warm Halloumi & Fennel Salad

The firm texture of halloumi cheese makes it perfect for the barbecue, as it keeps its shape very well. Combined with the delicate flavour of fennel, it makes a lovely chargrilled salad.

Serves 4
200g/7oz halloumi cheese, thickly sliced
2 fennel bulbs, trimmed and thinly sliced
30ml/2 tbsp roughly chopped fresh oregano
45ml/3 tbsp lemon-infused olive oil
salt and ground black pepper

1 Put the halloumi, fennel and oregano in a bowl and drizzle over the lemon-infused oil. Season with salt and black pepper to taste. (Halloumi is a fairly salty cheese, so be very careful when adding extra salt.)

2 Cover the bowl with clear film (plastic wrap) and chill for about 2 hours to allow the flavours to develop.

3 Place the halloumi and fennel on a griddle pan or over the barbecue, reserving the marinade, and cook for about 3 minutes on each side, until charred.

4 Divide the halloumi and fennel among four serving plates and drizzle over the reserved marinade. Serve immediately.

Halloumi & Grape Salad

Sweet, juicy grapes really complement the distinctive salty flavour of halloumi cheese in this delectable warm salad from Cyprus.

Serves 4
150g/5oz mixed green salad leaves
75g/3oz seedless green grapes
75g/3oz seedless black grapes
250g/9oz halloumi cheese

45ml/3 tbsp olive oil
fresh young thyme leaves or dill, to garnish

For the dressing
60ml/4 tbsp olive oil
15ml/1 tbsp lemon juice
2.5ml/½ tsp caster (superfine) sugar
15ml/1 tbsp chopped fresh thyme or dill
salt and ground black pepper

1 To make the dressing, mix together the olive oil, lemon juice and sugar. Season with salt and pepper to taste. Stir in the thyme or dill and set aside.

2 Toss together the salad leaves and the green and black grapes, then transfer to a large serving plate.

3 Thinly slice the cheese. Heat the oil in a large frying pan. Add the cheese and fry briefly until turning golden on the underside. Turn the cheese with a fish slice or metal spatula and cook the other side until golden.

4 Arrange the cheese on top of the salad. Pour over the dressing, garnish with thyme or dill and serve immediately.

Cook's Tips
• Most supermarkets sell ready-mixed bags of prepared salad leaves, which are ideal for use in this recipe. Experiment with various combinations to find the lettuce flavours that you like best. A mix of rocket (arugula), spinach and watercress is good. or try a mix with fresh herbs included.
• Halloumi cheese is now widely available from most large supermarkets and Greek delicatessens.

Warm halloumi & fennel salad: Energy 215kcal/889kJ; Protein 10.2g; Carbohydrate 1.8g, of which sugars 1.7g; Fat 18.6g, of which saturates 8.1g; Cholesterol 29mg; Calcium 205mg; Fibre 2.4g; Sodium 209mg
Halloumi & grape salad: Energy 365kcal/1513kJ; Protein 12.2g; Carbohydrate 7.2g, of which sugars 7.2g; Fat 32.2g, of which saturates 11.4g; Cholesterol 36mg; Calcium 250mg; Fibre 0.8g; Sodium 250mg

Fragrant Mushrooms in Lettuce Leaves

This quick and easy vegetable dish is served on lettuce leaf "saucers" so can be eaten with the fingers.

Serves 2

30ml/2 tbsp vegetable oil
2 garlic cloves, finely chopped
2 baby cos or romaine lettuces,
  or 2 Little Gem (Bibb) lettuces
1 lemon grass stalk,
  finely chopped
2 kaffir lime leaves, rolled in
  cylinders and thinly sliced
200g/7oz/3 cups oyster or
  chestnut mushrooms, sliced
1 small fresh red chilli, seeded
  and finely chopped
juice of ½ lemon
30ml/2 tbsp light soy sauce
5ml/1 tsp palm sugar (jaggery) or
  light muscovado (brown) sugar
1 small bunch fresh mint, leaves
  removed from the stalks

1 Heat the oil in a wok or frying pan. Add the garlic and cook over a medium heat, stirring occasionally, until golden. Do not let it burn or it will taste bitter.

2 Meanwhile, divide up the lettuces into separate, individual leaves and set aside.

3 Increase the heat under the wok or pan and add the lemon grass, lime leaves and mushrooms. Stir-fry for about 2 minutes.

4 Add the chilli, lemon juice, soy sauce and sugar to the wok or pan. Toss the mixture over the heat to combine the ingredients together, then stir-fry for a further 2 minutes.

5 Arrange the lettuce leaves on a large plate. Spoon a small amount of the mushroom mixture onto each leaf, top with a mint leaf and serve immediately.

Cook's Tip
If you can't find kaffir leaves, use freshly grated (shredded) lime rind instead.

Thai Asparagus

This is an excitingly different way of cooking asparagus. The crunchy texture is retained and the flavour is complemented by the addition of galangal and chilli.

Serves 4

350g/12oz asparagus stalks
30ml/2 tbsp vegetable oil
1 garlic clove, crushed
15ml/1 tbsp sesame
  seeds, toasted
2.5cm/1in piece fresh galangal,
  finely shredded
1 fresh red chilli, seeded and
  finely chopped
15ml/1 tbsp Thai fish sauce
15ml/1 tbsp light soy sauce
45ml/3 tbsp water
5ml/1 tsp palm sugar (jaggery) or
  light muscovado (brown) sugar

1 Snap the asparagus stalks. They will break naturally at the junction between the woody base and the more tender portion of the stalk. Discard the woody parts of the stems.

2 Heat the vegetable oil in a wok and stir-fry the garlic, sesame seeds and galangal for 3–4 seconds, until the garlic is just beginning to turn golden.

3 Add the asparagus stalks and chilli, toss to mix, then add the fish sauce, soy sauce, water and sugar. Using two spoons, toss over the heat for a further 2 minutes, or until the asparagus just begins to soften and the liquid is reduced by half.

4 Carefully transfer to a warmed platter and serve immediately.

Cook's Tip
Galangal root belongs to the ginger family but has a more aromatic flavour. The pinkish skin has distinctive rings on it.

Variation
Try this with broccoli or pak choi (bok choy). The sauce also works very well with green beans.

Fragrant mushrooms: Energy 162kcal/672kJ; Protein 4.6g; Carbohydrate 7.9g, of which sugars 6.3g; Fat 12.7g, of which saturates 1.6g; Cholesterol 0mg; Calcium 117mg; Fibre 2.9g; Sodium 549mg
Thai asparagus: Energy 99kcal/410kJ; Protein 3.4g; Carbohydrate 3.1g, of which sugars 3g; Fat 8.2g, of which saturates 1.1g; Cholesterol 0mg; Calcium 50mg; Fibre 1.8g; Sodium 269mg

Pak Choi with Lime Dressing

Pasta, Asparagus & Potato Salad

If you like your food hot and spicy, then this is the dish for you! The fiery flavours pack a punch.

Serves 4
30ml/2 tbsp oil
3 fresh red chillies, cut
 into thin strips
4 garlic cloves, thinly sliced

6 spring onions (scallions),
 sliced diagonally
2 pak choi (bok choy), shredded
15ml/1 tbsp crushed peanuts

For the dressing
30ml/2 tbsp fresh lime juice
15–30ml/1–2 tbsp Thai
 fish sauce
250ml/8fl oz/1 cup coconut milk

1 To make the dressing, put the lime juice and fish sauce in a bowl and mix well, then gradually whisk in the coconut milk until thoroughly combined.

2 Heat the oil in a wok and stir-fry the chillies for 2–3 minutes, until crisp. Transfer to a plate using a slotted spoon. Add the garlic to the wok and stir-fry for 30–60 seconds, until golden brown. Transfer to the plate.

3 Stir-fry the white parts of the spring onions for about 2–3 minutes, then add the green parts and stir-fry for 1 minute more. Transfer to the plate.

4 Bring a large pan of lightly salted water to the boil and add the pak choi. Stir twice, then drain immediately.

5 Place the pak choi in a large bowl, add the dressing and toss to mix. Spoon into a large serving bowl and sprinkle with the crushed peanuts and the stir-fried chilli mixture. Serve warm.

Cook's Tips
• *Thai fish sauce is traditionally used for this dressing, but if you are cooking for vegetarians, mushroom sauce is a suitable vegetarian alternative.*
• *If pak choi is unavailable, use Chinese cabbage instead.*

Made with whole-wheat pasta, this delicious salad is a real treat, especially when made with fresh asparagus just in season.

Serves 4
225g/8oz/2 cups dried
 whole-wheat pasta shapes
60ml/4 tbsp extra-virgin olive oil
350g/12oz baby new potatoes
225g/8oz asparagus
115g/4oz piece Parmesan cheese
salt and ground black pepper

1 Bring a large pan of salted water to the boil, add the pasta and cook according to the packet instructions, until *al dente*. Drain well and toss with the olive oil while the pasta is still warm. Season with salt and ground black pepper.

2 Cook the potatoes in boiling salted water for 15 minutes, or until tender. Drain and toss together with the pasta.

3 Trim any woody ends off the asparagus and halve the stalks if very long. Blanch in boiling salted water for 6 minutes, until bright green and still crunchy. Drain. Plunge into cold water to refresh. Drain and dry on kitchen paper.

4 Toss the asparagus with the potatoes and pasta, adjust the seasoning to taste and transfer to a shallow serving bowl. Using a vegetable peeler, shave the Parmesan over the salad.

Pak choi with lime dressing: Energy 104kcal/434kJ; Protein 3.3g; Carbohydrate 5.2g, of which sugars 4.8g; Fat 8g, of which saturates 1.2g; Cholesterol 0mg; Calcium 116mg; Fibre 1.5g; Sodium 408mg
Pasta salad: Energy 341kcal/1440kJ; Protein 9.5g; Carbohydrate 56.3g, of which sugars 3.2g; Fat 10.2g, of which saturates 1.4g; Cholesterol 0mg; Calcium 44mg; Fibre 3.1g; Sodium 288mg

Feta & Mint Potato Salad

The oddly named pink fir apple potatoes are perfect for this salad, and taste great with feta cheese, yogurt and fresh mint. This dish goes very well with salmon and roasted chicken.

Serves 4
500g/1¼ lb pink fir
*   apple potatoes*
90g/3½ oz feta cheese, crumbled

For the dressing
225g/8oz/1 cup natural
*   (plain) yogurt*
15g/½oz/ ½ cup fresh
*   mint leaves*
30ml/2 tbsp mayonnaise
salt and ground black pepper

1 Steam the potatoes over a pan of boiling water for about 20 minutes, until tender.

2 Meanwhile, make the dressing. Mix the yogurt and mint in a food processor and pulse until the mint leaves are finely chopped. Scrape the mixture into a small bowl, stir in the mayonnaise and season to taste with salt and pepper.

3 Drain the potatoes well and transfer them to a large bowl. Spoon the dressing over the potatoes and scatter the feta cheese on top. Serve immediately.

Cook's Tip
Pink fir apple potatoes have a smooth waxy texture and retain their shape when cooked. Charlotte, Belle de Fontenay and other special salad potatoes could be used instead.

Variations
• *Crumbled Kefalotiri or young Manchego could be used instead of the feta.*
• *For a richer dressing, use Greek (US strained plain) yogurt.*

Warm Potato Salad with Herbs

Toss the potatoes in the dressing as soon as possible, so the flavours are fully absorbed. Use the best olive oil for an authentic Mediterranean taste.

Serves 6
1kg/2¼lb waxy or salad potatoes
90ml/6 tbsp extra-virgin olive oil
juice of 1 lemon
1 garlic clove, very finely chopped
30ml/2 tbsp chopped fresh herbs
*   such as parsley, basil or thyme*
salt and ground black pepper
basil leaves, to garnish

1 Cook the potatoes in their skins in boiling salted water, or steam them until tender.

2 Meanwhile, make the dressing. Mix together the olive oil, lemon juice, garlic and herbs and season thoroughly.

3 Drain the potatoes and leave to cool slightly. When they are cool enough to handle, peel them. Cut the potatoes into chunks and place in a large bowl.

4 Pour the dressing over the potatoes while they are still warm and mix well.

5 Serve immediately, garnished with basil leaves and ground black pepper.

Feta & mint potato salad: Energy 229kcal/959kJ; Protein 8.7g; Carbohydrate 25g, of which sugars 6.3g; Fat 11.2g, of which saturates 4.4g; Cholesterol 22mg; Calcium 204mg; Fibre 1.3g; Sodium 419mg
Warm potato salad with herbs: Energy 218kcal/913kJ; Protein 3g; Carbohydrate 27g, of which sugars 2.3g; Fat 11.6g, of which saturates 1.7g; Cholesterol 0mg; Calcium 23mg; Fibre 2g; Sodium 21mg

New Potato & Quail's Egg Salad

Freshly cooked eggs and tender potatoes mix perfectly with the flavour of celery salt and the peppery-tasting rocket leaves.

Serves 6
900g/2lb new potatoes
50g/2oz/4 tbsp butter
15ml/1 tbsp snipped chives
a pinch of celery salt
a pinch of paprika
12 quail's eggs
a few rocket (arugula) leaves
salt and ground black pepper
snipped chives, to garnish

1 Boil the potatoes in a large pan of salted water for about 20 minutes or until tender.

2 Meanwhile, beat the butter and chives together with the celery salt and the paprika.

3 While the potatoes are cooking, boil the eggs for 3 minutes, then drain and plunge into a bowl of cold water. Peel the eggs under running water.

4 Arrange the rocket leaves on individual plates or a serving platter and top with the eggs.

5 Drain the potatoes and add the seasoned butter. Toss well to melt the butter and carefully spoon the potatoes onto the plates of rocket and egg. Garnish the salad with a few more snipped chives and serve immediately.

Cook's Tips
• *You can buy bags of rocket, on its own, or mixed with other leaves, in many supermarkets. It is also easy to grow from seed and makes a worthwhile addition to a herb patch.*
• *Tiny quail's eggs are available from larger supermarkets and butchers. They make an attractive addition to any salad. If unavailable, use hen's eggs, quartered.*

Warm Hazelnut & Pistachio Salad

Two kinds of crunchy nuts turn ordinary potato salad into a really special accompaniment. This would be lovely with cold sliced roast beef, tongue or ham, but you can also serve it on its own as a healthy snack.

Serves 4
900g/2lb small new or
* salad potatoes*
30ml/2 tbsp hazelnut or
* walnut oil*
60ml/4 tbsp sunflower oil
juice of 1 lemon
25g/1oz/¼ cup hazelnuts
15 pistachio nuts
salt and ground black pepper
flat leaf parsley sprig, to garnish

1 Cook the potatoes in their skins in boiling salted water for about 10–15 minutes until tender. Drain the potatoes well and leave to cool slightly.

2 Meanwhile, mix together the hazelnut or walnut oil with the sunflower oil and lemon juice. Season well with salt and ground black pepper.

3 Using a sharp knife, roughly chop the hazelnuts and pistachios.

4 Put the cooled potatoes in a large bowl and pour the dressing over. Toss to combine. Sprinkle the salad with the chopped nuts and serve immediately, garnished with parsley.

New potato & quail's egg salad: Energy 204kcal/855kJ; Protein 5.7g; Carbohydrate 24.2g, of which sugars 2g; Fat 10.1g, of which saturates 5.3g; Cholesterol 113mg; Calcium 25mg; Fibre 1.5g; Sodium 102mg
Warm hazelnut & pistachio salad: Energy 369kcal/1541kJ; Protein 5.4g; Carbohydrate 36.9g, of which sugars 3.4g; Fat 23.2g, of which saturates 2.6g; Cholesterol 0mg; Calcium 27mg; Fibre 2.9g; Sodium 45mg

Warm Potato Salad with Bacon Dressing

This tasty summer salad becomes a favourite with all who try it. Use real new-season potatoes rather than all-year "baby" potatoes, if possible, and also dry-cured bacon. Using superior ingredients makes this a special dish and it's ideal for outdoor eating or a party.

Serves 4–6
900g/2lb small new potatoes
1 fresh mint sprig
15–30ml/1–2 tbsp olive oil
1 onion, chopped
175g/6oz streaky (fatty) or back (lean) bacon, diced
2 garlic cloves, crushed
30ml/2 tbsp chopped parsley
1 small bunch chives, chopped
15ml/1 tbsp wine vinegar, or cider vinegar
15ml/1 tbsp wholegrain mustard
salt and ground black pepper

1 Scrape or rub off the skins from the new potatoes, and cook in salted water with the mint for about 10 minutes, or until just tender. Drain, cool a little, then turn into a salad bowl.

2 Heat the oil in a frying pan, then add the onion and cook gently until just softening. Add the diced bacon to the pan and cook for 3–5 minutes, until beginning to crisp up.

3 Add the crushed garlic and cook for another minute or so, and then add the chopped herbs, the vinegar and mustard. Season with salt and pepper to taste, remembering that the bacon may be quite salty.

4 Pour the dressing over the potatoes. Toss gently to mix, and serve warm.

> **Variation**
> Finely chopped spring onions (scallions) can replace the chopped chives and/or chopped parsley, if you like.

Curried Potato Salad with Mango Dressing

This sweet and spicy salad is a wonderful accompaniment to roasted meats.

Serves 4–6
900g/2lb new potatoes
15ml/1 tbsp olive oil
1 onion, sliced into rings
1 garlic clove, crushed
5ml/1 tsp ground cumin
5ml/1 tsp ground coriander
1 mango, peeled, stoned (pitted) and diced
30ml/2 tbsp demerara (raw) sugar
30ml/2 tbsp lime juice
15ml/1 tbsp sesame seeds
salt and ground black pepper
deep fried coriander (cilantro) leaves, to garnish

1 Cut the potatoes in half, then cook them in their skins in boiling salted water until tender. Drain well.

2 Heat the oil in a frying pan (skillet) and fry the onion and garlic over a low heat for 10 minutes until they start to brown.

3 Stir in the ground cumin and coriander and fry for a few seconds. Stir in the mango and sugar and fry for 5 minutes, until soft. Remove the pan from the heat and squeeze in the lime juice. Season with salt and pepper.

4 Place the potatoes in a large bowl and spoon the mango dressing over. Sprinkle with sesame seeds and serve while the dressing is still warm. Garnish with the coriander leaves.

> **Cook's Tip**
> To prepare the mango, cut through the mango lengthwise on either side of the stone (pit) to slice off two sections. Leaving the skin on each section, cross hatch the flesh, then bend it back so that the cubes stand proud of the skin. Slice them off with a small knife. Peel the remaining central section of the mango, then cut off the remaining flesh in chunks and dice.

Curried potato salad with mango: Energy 174kcal/737kJ; Protein 3.3g; Carbohydrate 33.7g, of which sugars 11.2g; Fat 3.8g, of which saturates 0.7g; Cholesterol 0mg; Calcium 34mg; Fibre 2.5g; Sodium 18mg
Warm potato salad: Energy 264Kcal/112kJ; Protein 13.3g; carbohydrate 39.9g, of which sugars 5.6g; Fat 6.8g, of which saturates 1.7g; Cholesterol 14mg; calcium 76mg; Fibre 4g; Sodium 625mg

Sweet Potato & Carrot Salad

This warm salad has a sweet-and-sour taste, and lots of contrasting texture.

Serves 4
1 medium sweet potato
2 carrots, cut into thick
  diagonal slices
3 tomatoes
75g/3oz/½ cup canned
  chickpeas, drained
8–10 iceberg lettuce leaves

For the dressing
15ml/1 tbsp clear honey
90ml/6 tbsp natural (plain) yogurt
2.5ml/½ tsp salt
5ml/1 tsp ground black pepper

For the garnish
15ml/1 tbsp walnuts
15ml/1 tbsp sultanas
  (golden raisins)
1 small onion, cut into rings

1 Peel the sweet potato and cut roughly into cubes. Boil it until it is soft but not mushy, then cover the pan and set aside.

2 Boil the carrots for just a few minutes, making sure that they remain crunchy. Drain both the carrots and sweet potato and place in a mixing bowl.

3 Slice the tops off the tomatoes, then scoop out the seeds with a spoon and discard. Roughly chop the tomato flesh. Add the chickpeas and tomatoes to the sweet potato and carrots and mix gently.

4 Slice the lettuce into strips across the leaves. Line a salad bowl with the lettuce. Place the sweet potato mixture on top.

5 To make the dressing, whisk together the honey, yogurt, salt and black pepper in a small bowl. Garnish the salad with the walnuts, sultanas and onion rings, then pour the dressing over the top just before serving.

Cook's Tip
This salad also makes an excellent lunch or supper dish when served with a sweet mango chutney and warm naan bread.

Baked Sweet Potato Salad

This salad has a truly tropical taste and is ideal served with Asian or Caribbean dishes.

Serves 4–6
1kg/2¼lb sweet potatoes
1 red (bell) pepper, seeded and
  finely diced
3 celery sticks, finely diced
¼ red onion, finely chopped
1 fresh red chilli, finely chopped

salt and ground black pepper
coriander (cilantro) leaves,
  to garnish

For the dressing
45ml/3 tbsp chopped fresh
  coriander (cilantro)
juice of 1 lime
150ml/¼ pint/⅔ cup natural
  (plain) yogurt

1 Preheat the oven to 200°C/400°F/Gas 6. Wash the potatoes, and pierce them all over with a fork. Place in the oven and bake for about 40 minutes, or until tender.

2 Meanwhile, make the dressing. Whisk together the coriander, lime juice and yogurt in a small bowl and season to taste with salt and pepper. Chill in the refrigerator while you prepare the remaining salad ingredients.

3 In a large bowl, mix the diced red pepper, celery, chopped onion and chilli together.

4 Remove the potatoes from the oven. As soon as they are cool enough to handle, peel them and cut them into cubes. Add them to the bowl. Drizzle the dressing over and toss carefully. Taste and adjust the seasoning, if necessary. Serve, garnished with coriander leaves.

Cook's Tip
It is generally thought that the seeds are the hottest part of a chilli. In fact, they contain no capsaicin – the hot element – but it is intensely concentrated in the flesh surrounding them. Removing the seeds usually removes this extra-hot flesh.

Baked sweet potato salad: Energy 176kcal/750kJ; Protein 4g; Carbohydrate 40.4g, of which sugars 14.1g; Fat 1g, of which saturates 0.3g; Cholesterol 0mg; Calcium 116mg; Fibre 5.2g; Sodium 103mg
Sweet potato & carrot salad: Energy 153kcal/648kJ; Protein 4.7g; Carbohydrate 26.7g, of which sugars 15.4g; Fat 3.9g, of which saturates 0.6g; Cholesterol 0mg; Calcium 88mg; Fibre 3.9g; Sodium 95mg

Glazed Sweet Potato

Smoky bacon is the perfect addition to these melt-in-the-mouth sugar-topped potatoes. They taste great as a change from regular roast potatoes with roast duck, pork or chicken.

45ml/3 tbsp butter
4 strips smoked lean bacon, cut
    into matchsticks
salt and ground black pepper
1 flat leaf parsley sprig,
    to garnish

Serves 4–6
butter, for greasing
900g/2lb sweet potatoes
115g/4oz/½ cup soft light
    brown sugar
30ml/2 tbsp lemon juice

1 Preheat the oven to 190°C/375°F/Gas 5 and lightly butter a shallow ovenproof dish. Cut each unpeeled sweet potato crosswise into three and cook in boiling water, covered, for about 25 minutes, until just tender.

2 Drain and leave to cool. When cool enough to handle, peel and slice thickly. Arrange in a single layer, overlapping the slices, in the prepared dish.

3 Sprinkle over the sugar and lemon juice and dot knobs of butter all over the surface.

4 Top with the bacon and season well. Bake uncovered for 35–40 minutes, basting once or twice.

5 The potatoes are ready once they are tender, test them with a knife to make sure. Remove from the oven once they are cooked.

6 Preheat the grill (broiler) to a high heat. Sprinkle the potatoes with parsley. Place the pan under the grill for 2–3 minutes, until the potatoes are browned and the bacon is crispy. Serve the dish piping hot.

Summer Vegetable Braise

Tender young vegetables are ideal for quick cooking in a minimum of liquid.

salt and ground black pepper
chopped fresh parsley and
    snipped fresh chives, to garnish

Serves 4
175g/6oz baby carrots
175g/6oz/1½ cups sugar snap
    peas or mangetouts
    (snow peas)
115g/4oz baby corn
90ml/6 tbsp vegetable stock
10ml/2 tsp lime juice

1 Place the baby carrots, peas and baby corn in a large heavy pan with the vegetable stock and lime juice. Bring to the boil.

2 Cover the pan and reduce the heat, then simmer for about 6–8 minutes, shaking the pan occasionally, until the vegetables are just tender.

3 Season the vegetables to taste with salt and pepper, then stir in the chopped fresh parsley and snipped fresh chives. Cook the vegetables for a few seconds more, stirring them once or twice until the herbs are well mixed, then serve.

Cook's Tip
This dish would be excellent for anyone on a low-fat diet.

Variations
• Mix and match the vegetables as you wish: asparagus and young broad (fava) beans would make good additions.
• You can cook a winter version of this dish using seasonal root vegetables. Cut the peeled vegetables into even-sized chunks and cook for slightly longer.

Glazed potato: Energy 298kcal/1258kJ; Protein 4.7g; Carbohydrate 52g, of which sugars 28.6g; Fat 9.4g, of which saturates 5.1g; Cholesterol 25mg; Calcium 48mg; Fibre 3.6g; Sodium 363mg
Summer braise: Energy 36kcal/151kJ; Protein 2.7g; Carbohydrate 5.9g, of which sugars 5.1g; Fat 0.3g, of which saturates 0.1g; Cholesterol 0mg; Calcium 33mg; Fibre 2.5g; Sodium 340mg

Fresh Tomato & Tarragon Salsa

Plum tomatoes, garlic, olive oil and balsamic vinegar make for a very Mediterranean salsa – try serving this with grilled lamb cutlets or toss it with freshly cooked pasta.

Serves 4
8 plum tomatoes, or 500g/1¼lb
   sweet cherry tomatoes

60ml/4 tbsp olive oil or
   sunflower oil
15ml/1 tbsp balsamic vinegar
30ml/2 tbsp chopped fresh
   tarragon, plus extra shredded
   leaves, to garnish
1 small garlic clove, finely
   chopped or crushed
salt and ground black pepper

1 Make a cut in the top of the tomatoes, then plunge into boiling water for 30 seconds. Remove with a slotted spoon and refresh in cold water.

2 Slip off the tomato skins. Halve the tomatoes, scoop out and discard the seeds, then finely dice the flesh.

3 Whisk together the oil and balsamic vinegar with plenty of salt and pepper. Add the chopped fresh tarragon to the dressing and whisk to mix.

4 Mix the tomatoes and garlic in a bowl and pour the tarragon dressing over. Stand for 1 hour to allow the flavours to blend, before serving at room temperature. Garnish with coarsely chopped tarragon.

> **Cook's Tip**
> Be sure to serve this salsa at room temperature as the tomatoes taste less sweet, and rather acidic, when chilled.

> **Variation**
> Use a finely chopped red onion instead of the garlic. Stand the onion in some lime juice to soften before adding to the salsa.

Smoky Tomato Salsa

The smoky flavour in this recipe comes from the smoked bacon and the barbecue marinade. Served with sour cream, this salsa makes a great baked potato filler.

Serves 4
450g/1lb tomatoes
4 rindless smoked streaky (fatty)
   bacon rashers (strips)

15ml/1 tbsp vegetable oil
45ml/3 tbsp chopped fresh
   coriander (cilantro) or
   parsley leaves
1 garlic clove, finely chopped
15ml/1 tbsp smoky (barbecue)
   marinade
juice of 1 lime
salt and ground black pepper

1 Make a cut in the top of the tomatoes, then plunge into boiling water for 30 seconds. Refresh in cold water, then remove the skins. Halve the tomatoes, scoop out and discard the seeds, then finely dice the flesh.

2 Cut the smoked bacon into small pieces. Heat the oil in a frying pan and cook the bacon for 5 minutes, stirring occasionally, until crisp and browned. Remove from the heat and drain on kitchen paper. Leave to cool for a few minutes, then place in a mixing bowl.

3 Add the finely diced tomatoes and the chopped fresh coriander or parsley to the bowl. Stir in the finely chopped garlic, then add the liquid smoke and freshly squeezed lime juice. Season the salsa with salt and pepper to taste and mix well, using a wooden spoon or plastic spatula.

4 Spoon the smoky salsa into a serving bowl, cover with clear film (plastic wrap) and chill until ready to serve.

> **Variation**
> Give this smoky salsa an extra kick by adding a dash of Tabasco sauce or a pinch of dried chilli flakes.

Smoky tomato salsa: Energy 99kcal/412kJ; Protein 5g; Carbohydrate 3.6g, of which sugars 3.6g; Fat 7.3g, of which saturates 2g; Cholesterol 13mg; Calcium 17mg; Fibre 1.3g; Sodium 396mg
Fresh tomato & tarragon salsa: Energy 124kcal/512kJ; Protein 1.2g; Carbohydrate 4.2g, of which sugars 4.1g; Fat 11.5g, of which saturates 1.7g; Cholesterol 0mg; Calcium 29mg; Fibre 1.8g; Sodium 15mg

Classic Tomato Salsa

A classic Mexican salsa, full of fiery flavour. Use three chillies for a milder taste, up to six if you like it hot.

Serves 6
3–6 fresh serrano chillies
I large white onion, finely chopped
grated (shredded) rind and juice of 2 limes, plus pared lime rind, to garnish
8 ripe, firm tomatoes
large bunch of fresh coriander (cilantro), chopped finely
1.5ml/¼ tsp caster (superfine) sugar
salt

I To peel the chillies, spear them on a long-handled metal skewer and roast them over the flame of a gas burner until the skins blister and darken. Do not let the flesh burn. Alternatively, dry fry them in a griddle pan until the skins are scorched.

2 Place the roasted chillies in a strong plastic bag and tie the top of the bag. Set aside for about 20 minutes. Meanwhile, put the onion in a bowl with the lime rind and juice. The lime juice will soften the onion.

3 Remove the chillies from the bag and peel off the skins. Cut off the stalks, then slit the chillies and scrape out the seeds. Chop the flesh roughly and set aside.

4 Make a cut in the top of the tomatoes, then plunge into boiling water for 30 seconds. Refresh in cold water. Remove the skins completely. Dice the tomato flesh and put in a bowl.

5 Add the softened onion and lime juice mixture to the tomatoes, together with the coriander, chillies and the sugar. Mix gently until the sugar has dissolved. Cover and chill for 2–3 hours to allow the flavours to blend. Garnish with lime to serve.

Variation
Use spring onions (scallions) instead of white onion. For a smoky flavour use chipotle chillies instead of serrano chillies.

Fragrant Roasted Tomato Salsa

Roasting the tomatoes gives a greater depth to the flavour of this salsa, which also benefits from the warm, rounded flavour of roasted chillies. This salad is a classic accompaniment to tortillas and other Mexican dishes.

Serves 6
500g/1¼lb tomatoes, preferably beefsteak tomatoes
2 fresh Serrano chillies or other fresh red chillies
I onion
juice of I lime
I large bunch fresh coriander (cilantro)
salt

I Preheat the oven to 200°C/400°F/Gas 6. Cut the tomatoes into quarters and place them in a roasting pan. Add the chillies and roast for 45 minutes to I hour, until the tomatoes and chillies are charred and softened.

2 Place the roasted chillies in a strong plastic bag. Tie the top to keep the steam in and set aside for 20 minutes. Leave the tomatoes to cool slightly, then use a small, sharp knife to remove the skins and dice the flesh.

3 Chop the onion finely, then place it in a bowl and add the lime juice and the diced tomatoes. Mix well.

4 Remove the chillies from the bag and peel off the skins. Cut off the stalks, then slit the chillies and scrape out the seeds with a sharp knife. Chop the chillies roughly and add them to the onion mixture. Mix well to combine.

5 Chop the coriander and add most of it to the salsa. Add salt to season, cover and chill for at least I hour before serving, sprinkled with the remaining chopped coriander.

Cook's Tip
This salsa will keep for a week in the refrigerator. It is a useful condiment for adding punchy flavour to a meal.

Classic tomato salsa: Energy 45kcal/190kJ; Protein 2.2g; Carbohydrate 8.2g, of which sugars 7g; Fat 0.7g, of which saturates 0.1g; Cholesterol 0mg; Calcium 43mg; Fibre 2.3g; Sodium 16mg
Fragrant roasted tomato salsa: Energy 22kcal/95kJ; Protein 1.2g; Carbohydrate 3.7g, of which sugars 3.4g; Fat 0.4g, of which saturates 0.1g; Cholesterol 0mg; Calcium 28mg; Fibre 1.4g; Sodium 11mg

Bloody Mary Salsa

Serve this perfect party salsa with sticks of crunchy celery or fingers of cucumber or, on a really special occasion, with freshly shucked oysters.

Serves 2
4 ripe tomatoes
1 celery stick
1 garlic clove

2 spring onions (scallions)
45ml/3 tbsp tomato juice
Worcestershire sauce, to taste
Tabasco sauce, to taste
10ml/2 tsp horseradish sauce
15ml/1 tbsp vodka
1 lemon
salt and ground black pepper

1 Halve the tomatoes, celery and garlic. Trim the spring onions.

2 Put the tomatoes, celery, garlic and spring onions in a blender or food processor. Process until finely chopped, then transfer the vegetable mixture to a serving bowl.

3 Stir in the tomato juice, a little at a time, then add a few drops of Worcestershire sauce and Tabasco sauce to taste. Mix well and set aside for 10–15 minutes.

4 Stir in the horseradish sauce and vodka. Squeeze the lemon and stir the juice into the salsa. Add salt and pepper to taste. Serve immediately, or cover and chill for 1–2 hours.

Cook's Tip
This is based on the famous Bloody Mary cocktail. To make the drink, mix 1 measure of vodka to 2 of tomato juice, with a dash of Tabasco and Worcestershire sauce, lemon juice and ice.

Variation
Blend 1–2 chopped, seeded, fresh red chillies with the tomatoes, instead of stirring in the Tabasco sauce.

Grilled Corn-on-the-Cob Salsa

This is an unusual salsa, made with deliciously sweet vegetables. Use cherry tomatoes for an extra special flavour, and combine with the ripest and freshest corn on the cob.

Serves 4
2 corn on the cob
30ml/2 tbsp melted butter
4 tomatoes
8 spring onions (scallions)
1 garlic clove, crushed
30ml/2 tbsp fresh lemon juice
30ml/2 tbsp olive oil
Tabasco sauce, to taste
salt and ground black pepper

1 Remove the husks and silky threads covering the corn on the cob. Brush the cobs with the melted butter and gently cook on the barbecue or grill (broil) them for 20–30 minutes, turning occasionally, until tender and tinged brown.

2 To remove the kernels, stand each cob upright on a chopping board and use a large, heavy knife to slice down the length of the cob and scrape off the kernels.

3 Make a cut in the top of the tomatoes, then plunge into boiling water for 30 seconds. Refresh in cold water, then slip off the skins and dice the tomato flesh.

4 Place 6 spring onions on a chopping board and chop finely. Mix with the garlic, corn and tomato in a small bowl.

5 Stir the lemon juice and olive oil together, adding Tabasco sauce, salt and pepper to taste. Pour this mixture over the salsa and stir well. Cover the salsa and leave at room temperature for 1–2 hours before serving, to allow the flavours to blend. Garnish with the remaining spring onions.

Cook's Tip
Make this colourful salsa in summer when fresh, ripe cobs of corn are readily available in the shops.

Bloody Mary salsa: Energy 58kcal/243kJ; Protein 1.6g; Carbohydrate 6.9g, of which sugars 6.7g; Fat 1g, of which saturates 0.3g; Cholesterol 1mg; Calcium 23mg; Fibre 2.2g; Sodium 88mg
Grilled corn-on-the-cob salsa: Energy 249kcal/1044kJ; Protein 4.1g; Carbohydrate 30.4g, of which sugars 13.3g; Fat 13.3g, of which saturates 5g; Cholesterol 16mg; Calcium 20mg; Fibre 2.7g; Sodium 326mg

Orange, Tomato & Chive Salsa

Fresh chives and sweet oranges provide a very cheerful combination of flavours. This fruity salsa is very good served alongside other salads.

Serves 4
2 large, sweet oranges
1 beefsteak tomato, or
  2 plum tomatoes
bunch of fresh chives
1 garlic clove
30ml/2 tbsp extra-virgin olive oil
  or grapeseed oil
sea salt

1 Slice the base off 1 orange so that it will stand firmly on a chopping board. Using a large sharp knife, remove the peel by slicing from the top to the bottom of the orange. Repeat with the second orange.

2 Working over a bowl to catch the juice, cut the segments away from the membranes in each orange: slice towards the middle of the fruit, and slightly to one side of a segment, and then gently twist the knife to release the orange segment. Squeeze any juice from the remaining membrane.

3 Roughly chop the orange segments and add them to the bowl with the collected orange juice. Halve the tomato and use a teaspoon to scoop the seeds into the bowl. With a sharp knife, finely dice the tomato flesh and add to the oranges and juice in the bowl.

4 Hold the bunch of chives neatly together and use a pair of kitchen scissors to snip them into the bowl.

5 Thinly slice the garlic and stir it into the orange mixture. Pour the olive oil over the salad, season with sea salt and stir well to mix. Serve the salsa within 2 hours.

> **Variation**
> Add a sprinkling of chopped pistachios or toasted pine nuts.

Fiery Salsa

This is a scorchingly hot salsa for only the very brave! Spread it sparingly on to cooked meats and burgers or add a tiny amount to a curry or pot of chilli.

Serves 4–6
6 Scotch bonnet chillies
2 ripe tomatoes
4 standard green jalapeño chillies
30ml/2 tbsp chopped fresh
  parsley
30ml/2 tbsp olive oil
15ml/1 tbsp balsamic vinegar or
  sherry vinegar
salt

1 Skin the Scotch bonnet chillies, either by holding them in a gas flame for 3 minutes until the skin blackens and blisters, or by plunging them into boiling water. Then, using rubber gloves, rub off the skin from the chilli.

2 Hold each tomato in a gas flame for 3 minutes until the skin starts to come away, or plunge them into a bowl of boiling water. Remove the skins, halve the tomatoes, and remove the seeds. Chop the flesh very finely.

3 Try not to touch the Scotch bonnet chillies with your bare hands: use a fork to hold them and slice them open with a knife. Scrape out and discard the seeds. Finely chop the flesh.

4 Halve the jalapeño chillies, remove their seeds and finely slice them widthways into tiny strips. Mix both types of chillies, the tomatoes and the chopped parsley in a bowl.

5 In a small bowl, whisk the olive oil with the vinegar and a little salt. Pour this over the salsa and cover the dish. Chill before serving. The salsa will store for up to 3 days in the refrigerator.

> **Cook's Tip**
> If you have to touch the chillies with your hands, wear protective gloves. Do not touch your eyes when handling chillies.

Orange, tomato & chive salsa: Energy 91kcal/380kJ; Protein 1.3g; Carbohydrate 9.3g, of which sugars 9.3g; Fat 5.7g, of which saturates 0.8g; Cholesterol 0mg; Calcium 49mg; Fibre 2g; Sodium 7mg
Fiery salsa: Energy 42kcal/173kJ; Protein 0.7g; Carbohydrate 1.1g, of which sugars 1g; Fat 3.9g, of which saturates 0.6g; Cholesterol 0mg; Calcium 21mg; Fibre 0.7g; Sodium 6mg

Sweet Potato Salsa

Eye-catchingly colourful and delightfully sweet, this delicious salsa makes the perfect accompaniment to hot, spicy Mexican dishes.

Serves 4
675g/1½lb sweet potatoes
juice of 1 small orange
5ml/1 tsp crushed dried
   jalapeño chillies
4 small spring onions (scallions)
juice of 1 small lime (optional)
salt

1 Peel the sweet potatoes and dice the flesh finely. Bring a pan of water to the boil. Add the sweet potato and cook for 8–10 minutes, until just soft.

2 Drain off the cooking water from the sweet potato, cover the pan and put it back on the hob, having first turned off the heat. Leave the sweet potato for about 5 minutes to dry out, then transfer to a bowl and set aside.

3 Mix the orange juice and crushed dried chillies in a bowl. Chop the spring onions finely and add them to the orange juice and chilli mixture.

4 When the sweet potato is cool, add the orange juice mixture and toss carefully until all the pieces are coated.

5 Cover the bowl and chill for at least 1 hour, then taste and season with salt. Stir in the lime juice if you prefer a fresher taste to the salsa.

Cook's Tips
• This fresh and tasty salsa is also very good served with a simple grilled salmon fillet or other fish dishes, and makes a delicious accompaniment to veal escalopes or grilled chicken.
• The salsa will keep for 2–3 days in a covered bowl in the refrigerator. Leaving the salsa to stand in this way will also help the flavours to develop.

Mexican Nopales Salsa

Nopales are the fleshy leaves of an edible cactus. Fresh nopales are hard to find outside Mexico, so look out for the canned version.

Serves 4
2 fresh red chillies
250g/9oz nopales (cactus paddles)
3 spring onions (scallions)
3 garlic cloves, peeled
½ red onion, chopped finely
100g/3½ oz fresh tomatillos,
   chopped finely
2.5ml/½ tsp salt
150ml/¼ pint/⅔ cup
   cider vinegar

1 Spear the chillies on a long-handled metal skewer and roast them over the flame of a gas burner (or under the grill) until the skins blister and darken. Do not let the flesh burn. Place the roasted chillies in a strong plastic bag and tie the top.

2 After 20 minutes, remove the chillies from the bag and peel off the skins. Cut off the stalks, then slit the chillies and scrape out the seeds. Chop the chillies roughly and set them aside.

3 Carefully remove the thorns from the nopales. Wearing gloves or holding each cactus paddle in turn with kitchen tongs, cut off the bumps that contain the thorns with a sharp knife.

4 Cut off and discard the thick base from each cactus paddle. Rinse the paddles well and cut them into strips then cut the strips into small pieces.

5 Bring a large pan of lightly salted water to the boil. Add the cactus strips, spring onions and garlic. Boil for 10–15 minutes, until the cactus is just tender. Drain the mixture, rinse under cold running water to remove any remaining stickiness, then drain again. Discard the spring onions and garlic.

6 Place the red onion and tomatillos in a bowl and add the cactus and chillies. Spoon into a large preserving jar, add the salt, pour in the vinegar and seal. Chill for at least 1 day, turning the jar occasionally to ensure that the nopales are marinated. The salsa will keep in the refrigerator for up to 10 days.

Black Bean Salsa

This salsa has a very striking appearance with its black colouring. Leave the salad for a day or two after making to allow the flavours to develop fully.

Serves 4

130g/4½ oz/generous ½ cup
   black beans, soaked overnight
   in water to cover

1 pasado chilli
2 fresh red fresno chillies
1 red onion, finely chopped
grated (shredded) rind and juice
   of 1 lime
30ml/2 tbsp Mexican beer
15ml/1 tbsp olive oil
1 small bunch fresh coriander
   (cilantro), chopped
salt

1 Drain the beans and put them in a large pan. Pour in water to cover and place the lid on the pan. Bring to the boil, lower the heat slightly and simmer the beans for about 40 minutes or until tender. They should still have a little bite and should not have begun to disintegrate.

2 Drain, rinse under cold water, then drain again and leave the beans until cold.

3 Soak the pasado chilli in hot water for about 10 minutes until softened. Drain, remove the stalk, then slit the chilli and scrape out the seeds with a small sharp knife. Chop the flesh finely.

4 Spear the fresno chillies on a long-handled metal skewer and roast them over the flame of a gas burner until the skins blister and darken. Do not let the flesh burn. Alternatively, dry-fry them in a griddle pan until the skins are scorched. Then place the roasted chillies in a strong plastic bag and tie the top to keep the steam in. Set aside for 20 minutes.

5 Remove the chillies from the bag and peel off the skins. Slit them, remove the seeds and chop them finely.

6 Transfer the beans to a bowl and add the onion and both types of chilli. Stir in the lime rind and juice, beer, oil and coriander. Season with salt and mix well. Chill before serving.

Pinto Bean Salsa

The beans give this authentic Mexican salsa a pretty, speckled look. The smoky flavour of the chipotle chillies and the herby taste of the pasilla chilli contrast well with the tart tomatillos. Unusually, these are not cooked.

Serves 4

130g/4½ oz/generous ½ cup
   pinto beans, soaked overnight
   in water to cover
2 chipotle chillies
1 pasilla chilli
2 garlic cloves, peeled
½ onion
200g/7oz fresh tomatillos
salt

1 Drain the beans and put them in a large pan. Pour in water to cover and place the lid on the pan. Bring to the boil, lower the heat slightly and simmer the beans for 45–50 minutes or until tender. They should still have a little bite and should not have begun to disintegrate.

2 Drain, rinse under cold water, then drain again and turn into a bowl. Leave the beans until cold.

3 Soak the chipotle and pasilla chillies in hot water for about 10 minutes until softened. Drain, reserving the soaking water. Remove the stalks, then slit each chilli and scrape out the seeds with a small sharp knife. Chop the flesh finely and mix it to a smooth paste with a little of the soaking water.

4 Roast the garlic in a dry frying pan over a medium heat for a few minutes until the cloves starts to turn golden. Crush them, then add to the beans.

5 Chop the onion and tomatillos and stir into the beans. Add the chilli paste and mix well. Add salt to taste, cover and chill.

> **Cook's Tip**
> Canned tomatillos can be used, but to keep a clean, fresh flavour add a little lime juice.

Onion Relish

This fiery side dish from Mexico is particularly good served with chicken, turkey or fish dishes.

Makes 1 small jar
2 fresh red fresno chillies
5ml/1 tsp allspice berries
2.5ml/½ tsp black peppercorns
5ml/1 tsp dried oregano
2 white onions
2 garlic cloves, peeled
100ml/3½fl oz/⅓ cup white wine vinegar
200ml/7fl oz/scant 1 cup cider vinegar
salt

1 Spear the fresno chillies on a long-handled metal skewer and roast them over the flame of a gas burner until the skins blister. Do not let the flesh burn. Alternatively, dry-fry them in a griddle pan until the skins are scorched. Place the roasted chillies in a strong plastic bag and tie the top. Set aside for 20 minutes.

2 Meanwhile, place the allspice, black peppercorns and oregano in a mortar or food processor. Grind slowly by hand with a pestle or process until coarsely ground.

3 Cut the onions in half and slice them thinly. Put them in a bowl. Dry roast the garlic in a heavy-based frying pan until golden, then crush and add to the onions in the bowl.

4 Remove the chillies from the bag and peel off the skins. Slit the chillies, scrape out the seeds, then chop them.

5 Add the ground spices to the onion mixture, followed by the chillies. Stir in both vinegars. Add salt to taste and mix thoroughly. Cover the bowl and chill in the refrigerator for at least 1 day before serving.

> **Cook's Tip**
> *White onions have a pungent flavour and are good in this salsa. Spanish onions can also be used. Shallots also make an excellent pickle.*

Chilli Strips with Lime

This fresh, tangy relish is ideal for serving with stews, rice dishes or bean dishes. The oregano adds a sweet note and the absence of sugar or oil makes this a very healthy choice.

Makes about 60ml/4 tbsp
10 fresh green chillies
½ white onion
4 limes
2.5ml/½ tsp dried oregano
salt

1 Roast the chillies in a griddle pan over a medium heat until the skins are charred and blistered. The flesh should not be allowed to blacken as this might make the salsa bitter. Place the roasted chillies in a strong plastic bag and tie the top to keep the steam in. Set aside for 20 minutes.

2 Meanwhile, slice the onion very thinly and put it in a large bowl. Squeeze the limes over a sieve (strainer) and add the juice to the bowl, with any pulp that gathers in the sieve. The lime juice will soften the onion. Stir in the oregano.

3 Remove the chillies from the bag and peel off the skins. Slit them, scrape out the seeds with a small sharp knife, then cut the chillies into long strips, which are called "rajas".

4 Add the chilli strips to the onion mixture and season with salt. Cover the bowl and chill for at least 1 day before serving, to allow the flavours to develop.

> **Cook's Tips**
> *• This method of roasting chillies in a griddle pan is ideal if you need more than one or two chillies, or if you do not have a gas burner. If you prefer to roast the chillies over a burner, spear the chillies, four or five at a time, on a long-handled metal skewer and hold them over the flame until the skins begin to blister. Take care not to let them burn.*
> *• This salsa will keep for up to 2 weeks in a covered bowl in the refrigerator. Use to add fiery flavour to a meal.*

Jicama Salsa

The jicama from Mexico, makes an unusual salsa with a delicious texture. Look out for this root vegetable in ethnic food stores.

Serves 4
1 small red onion
juice of 2 limes
3 small oranges
1 jicama, about 450g/1lb
1/2 cucumber
1 fresh red fresno chilli

1 Cut the onion in half, then slice each half finely. Place in a bowl, add the lime juice and leave to soak while you prepare the remaining ingredients.

2 Slice the top and bottom off each orange. Stand an orange on a board, then carefully slice off all the peel and pith. Hold the orange over a bowl and cut between the membranes so that the segments fall into the bowl. Squeeze the pulp over the bowl to extract the remaining juice.

3 Peel the jicama and rinse it in cold water. Cut it into quarters, then slice finely. Add to the bowl of orange juice.

4 Cut the unpeeled cucumber in half lengthwise, then use a teaspoon to scoop out the seeds. Slice the cucumber and add to the bowl. Remove the stalk from the chilli, slit it open and scrape out the seeds with a small sharp knife. Chop the flesh finely and add to the bowl.

5 Add the sliced onion to the bowl, with any remaining lime juice, and mix well. Cover and leave to stand at room temperature for at least 1 hour before serving. If not serving immediately, chill in the refrigerator for up to 3 days.

Cook's Tip
The jicama is a round, brown root vegetable with a texture somewhere between that of water chestnut and crisp apple. It can be eaten raw or cooked, and is always peeled.

Chayote Salsa

You can't get more Mexican than this salsa. The main ingredient, chayote – or vegetable pear as it is sometimes called – tastes rather like cucumber and makes a refreshing salsa. The contrast between the crisp chayote, cool melon and hot habañero sauce is stunning.

Serves 6
1 chayote, about 200g/7oz
1/2 small Galia melon
10ml/2 tsp habañero sauce or similar hot chilli sauce
juice of 1 lime
2.5ml/1/2 tsp salt
2.5ml/1/2 tsp sugar

1 Peel the chayote, then cut slices of flesh away from the stone. Cut the slices into thin strips. Cut the melon in half, scoop the seeds out, and cut each half into two pieces. Remove the skin and cut the flesh into small cubes. Place in a bowl with the chayote strips.

2 Mix the chilli sauce, lime juice, salt and sugar in a bowl. Stir until all the sugar has dissolved. Pour over the melon and chayote mixture and mix thoroughly. Chill for at least 1 hour before serving, or keep for up to 3 days in the refrigerator.

Cook's Tip
The chayote is a gourd-like fruit, shaped like a large pear. Several varieties grow in Mexico, the most common being white-fleshed and smooth-skinned, with a taste reminiscent of cucumber. Chayotes should be peeled before being eaten raw or cooked. The seed, which looks rather like a large, flat almond, is edible. In some countries, chayotes are called christophenes or choko. They are also used in Chinese cooking, so will be found in Oriental stores.

Variation
For extra colour, add finely diced red (bell) pepper or tomato.

Aromatic Guacamole

Guacamole is often served as a first course with corn chips for dipping. This chunky version is a great accompaniment for grilled fish, poultry or meat, especially steak.

Serves 4

2 large ripe avocados
1 small red onion, very
    finely chopped
1 red or green chilli, seeded and
    very finely chopped
1/2–1 garlic clove, crushed with
    a little salt (see Cook's Tip)
finely grated (shredded) rind of 1/2
    lime and juice of 1–1 1/2 limes
pinch of sugar
225g/8oz tomatoes, seeded
    and chopped
30ml/2 tbsp roughly chopped
    fresh coriander (cilantro)
2.5–5ml/1/2–1 tsp ground toasted
    cumin seeds
15ml/1 tbsp olive oil
15–30ml/1–2 tbsp sour cream
    (optional)
salt and ground black pepper
lime wedges dipped in sea salt,
    and fresh coriander (cilantro)
    sprigs, to garnish

1 Cut 1 avocado in half and remove the stone (pit). Scrape the flesh from both halves into a bowl and mash roughly with a fork.

2 Stir in the onion, chilli, garlic, lime rind, sugar, tomatoes and coriander. Add the ground cumin and season with salt and pepper to taste, then stir in the olive oil.

3 Halve and stone (pit) the remaining avocado. Dice the flesh and stir it into the guacamole.

4 Squeeze in fresh lime juice to taste, mix well, then cover and leave to stand for 15 minutes so that the flavour develops. Stir in the soured cream, if using. Serve with lime wedges dipped in sea salt, and fresh coriander sprigs.

> **Cook's Tip**
> To crush garlic, place a peeled clove on a chopping board and chop it roughly. Sprinkle over a little sea salt and, using the flat side of a large knife blade, gradually work the salt into the garlic.

Onion, Mango & Peanut Chaat

Chaats are spiced relishes of vegetables and nuts served with Indian meals. Amchoor (mango powder) adds a deliciously fruity sourness to this mixture of onions and mango.

Serves 4

90g/3 1/2oz/scant 1 cup
    unsalted peanuts
15ml/1 tbsp peanut oil
1 onion, chopped
10cm/4in piece cucumber, seeded
    and cut into 5mm/1/4in dice
1 mango, peeled, stoned (pitted)
    and diced
1 green chilli, seeded and chopped
30ml/2 tbsp chopped fresh
    coriander (cilantro)
15ml/1 tbsp chopped fresh mint
15ml/1 tbsp lime juice
pinch of light muscovado
    (brown) sugar

For the chaat masala
10ml/2 tsp ground toasted
    cumin seeds
2.5ml/1/2 tsp cayenne pepper
5ml/1 tsp mango powder
    (amchoor)
2.5ml/1/2 tsp garam masala
pinch of ground asafoetida
salt and ground black pepper

1 To make the chaat masala, grind all the spices together, then season with 2.5ml/1/2 tsp each of salt and pepper.

2 Fry the peanuts in the oil until lightly browned, then drain on kitchen paper until cool.

3 Put the onion in a mixing bowl with the cucumber, mango, chilli, fresh coriander and mint. Sprinkle in 5ml/1 tsp of the chaat masala. Stir in the peanuts and then add lime juice and/or sugar to taste. Set the mixture aside for 20–30 minutes for the flavours to develop.

4 Turn the mixture into a serving bowl, sprinkle another 5ml/1 tsp of the chaat masala over and serve.

> **Cook's Tip**
> Any remaining chaat masala can be put in a sealed jar and kept for 4–6 weeks.

Aromatic guacamole: Energy 182kcal/752kJ; Protein 2.4g; Carbohydrate 4.7g, of which sugars 3.3g; Fat 17.1g, of which saturates 3.5g; Cholesterol 0mg; Calcium 41mg; Fibre 4g; Sodium 14mg
Onion, mango & peanut chaat: Energy 189kcal/788kJ; Protein 6.9g; Carbohydrate 9.8g, of which sugars 6.6g; Fat 14g, of which saturates 2.4g; Cholesterol 0mg; Calcium 41mg; Fibre 2.4g; Sodium 4mg

Quick-pickled Red Onions with Dill, Coriander & Juniper

Mild red onions are best for this quick pickle, which is based on a traditional Mexican method of pickling onions that was popularized by American cook Deborah Maddison. The pickle will keep in a covered jar in the refrigerator for up to one week, and is just the thing for adding a burst of flavour to a bland dish.

Serves 6
500g/1¼lb red onions, thinly sliced
250ml/8fl oz/1 cup rice wine vinegar or tarragon vinegar
5ml/1 tsp salt
15ml/1 tbsp caster (superfine) sugar
6 juniper berries, lightly crushed
30ml/2 tbsp chopped fresh dill
15ml/1 tbsp coriander seeds, bruised

1 Place the onions in a large bowl and pour over sufficient boiling water to cover. Immediately turn the onions into a colander, then set aside and allow to drain completely. Return the onions to the dried bowl.

2 In another bowl, mix together the vinegar, salt, sugar, juniper berries and chopped dill.

3 Heat the coriander seeds in a dry frying pan until they give off their aroma. Add the the toasted seeds to the vinegar mixture and stir. Pour the spiced vinegar over the onions, toss to mix, then leave to stand at room temperature for 1 hour. Drain before serving.

Variation
To make quick Mexican red onions, blanch 1 large sliced red onion, then toss with 5ml/1 tsp sugar and 105ml/7 tbsp lime juice or rice wine vinegar and a little finely chopped red or green chilli. Leave for 2–3 hours before draining, then season and serve. These onions are very good drained, then tossed with thinly sliced salted cucumber.

Tsatziki

Cool, creamy and refreshing, tzatziki is wonderfully easy to make and even easier to eat. Serve this classic Greek dip with toasted pitta bread as part of a salad spread, or with chargrilled vegetables.

Serves 4
1 mini cucumber, topped and tailed
4 spring onions (scallions)
1 garlic clove
200ml/7fl oz/scant 1 cup Greek (US strained plain) yogurt
45ml/3 tbsp chopped fresh mint
salt and ground black pepper
fresh mint sprig, to garnish
toasted pitta bread, to serve

1 Cut the cucumber into 5mm/¼in dice. Chop the spring onions and garlic very finely.

2 Beat the yogurt in a bowl until smooth, if necessary, then gently stir in the cucumber, spring onions, garlic and mint.

3 Add salt and plenty of ground black pepper to taste, then transfer the mixture to a serving bowl. Cover and chill in the refrigerator until ready to serve. Garnish with a mint sprig and serve with pitta bread.

Cook's Tip
Choose Greek-style (US strained plain) yogurt for this dip – it has a higher fat content than most yogurts, which gives the dish a deliciously rich, creamy texture.

Variation
A similar, but smoother, dip can be made in the food processor. Peel one mini cucumber and process with two garlic cloves and 75g/3oz/3 cups mixed fresh herbs to a purée. Stir the purée into 200ml/7fl oz/scant 1 cup soured cream and season to taste with salt and pepper.

Quick-pickled red onions: Energy 50kcal/209kJ; Protein 1.6g; Carbohydrate 10.3g, of which sugars 7.5g; Fat 0.6g, of which saturates 0.1g; Cholesterol 0mg; Calcium 43mg; Fibre 1.6g; Sodium 6mg
Tsatziki: Energy 67kcal/279kJ; Protein 4g; Carbohydrate 2.3g, of which sugars 1.6g; Fat 5.3g, of which saturates 2.6g; Cholesterol 0mg; Calcium 107mg; Fibre 0.3g; Sodium 39mg

Coconut Chutney with Onion & Chilli

Serve this exotic chutney as an accompaniment for Indian-style dishes or with a raita and other chutneys and poppadums as an interesting start to a meal.

Serves 4–6

200g/7oz fresh coconut, grated (shredded)
3–4 green chillies, seeded and chopped
20g/³⁄₄oz fresh coriander (cilantro), chopped
30ml/2 tbsp chopped fresh mint
30–45ml/2–3 tbsp lime juice
about 2.5ml/¹⁄₂ tsp salt
about 2.5ml/¹⁄₂ tsp caster (superfine) sugar
15–30ml/1–2 tbsp coconut milk (optional)
30ml/2 tbsp groundnut oil
5ml/1 tsp kalonji
1 small onion, very finely chopped
fresh coriander (cilantro) sprigs, to garnish

1 Place the coconut, chillies, coriander and mint in a food processor. Add 30ml/2 tbsp of the lime juice, then process until thoroughly chopped.

2 Scrape the mixture into a bowl and add more lime juice to taste. Add salt and sugar to taste. If the mixture is dry, stir in 15–30ml/1–2 tbsp coconut milk.

3 Heat the groundnut oil in a small pan and fry the kalonji until they begin to pop, then reduce the heat and add the onion. Fry, stirring frequently, for 4–5 minutes, until the onion softens but does not brown.

4 Stir the onion mixture into the coconut mixture and leave to cool. Garnish with coriander before serving.

> **Cook's Tips**
> • *Kalonji are small black seeds which have a slightly bitter, yet pleasant, taste. They are fried to release their flavour.*
> • *Add more chillies if you prefer a chutney with a hotter flavour.*

Green Vegetable Salad with Coconut Mint Dip

This is traditionally served with Malaysian meat dishes.

Serves 4–6

115g/4oz mangetouts (snow peas), halved
115g/4oz green beans, halved
¹⁄₂ cucumber, peeled, halved and sliced
115g/4oz Chinese leaves (Chinese cabbage), roughly shredded
115g/4oz beansprouts
salt

For the dressing
1 garlic clove, crushed
1 small fresh green chilli, seeded and finely chopped
10ml/2 tsp sugar
45ml/3 tbsp creamed coconut
75ml/5 tbsp boiling water
10ml/2 tsp fish sauce
45ml/3 tbsp vegetable oil
juice of 1 lime
30ml/2 tbsp chopped fresh mint

1 Bring a pan of lightly salted water to the boil. Blanch the mangetouts, green beans, beansprouts and cucumber for 4 minutes. Drain, refresh under cold water and drain again.

2 To make the dressing, pound the garlic, chilli and sugar together in a mortar with a pestle. Add the creamed coconut, water, fish sauce, vegetable oil, lime juice and mint. Stir well.

3 Arrange the blanched vegetables, Chinese leaves and beansprouts on a bed of lettuce in a basket. Pour the dressing into a shallow bowl and serve immediately.

> **Cook's Tip**
> *Creamed coconut is sold in blocks from most supermarkets.*

> **Variation**
> *Vary the vegetables as you like – carrot sticks and red (bell) pepper strips would make a colourful addition.*

Coconut chutney: Energy 145kcal/596kJ; Protein 1.6g; Carbohydrate 2.8g, of which sugars 2.5g; Fat 14.2g, of which saturates 9.3g; Cholesterol 0mg; Calcium 40mg; Fibre 3.3g; Sodium 11mg
Green vegetable salad: Energy 128kcal/530kJ; Protein 2.4g; Carbohydrate 5.2g, of which sugars 4.5g; Fat 11g, of which saturates 5.2g; Cholesterol 0mg; Calcium 31mg; Fibre 1.4g; Sodium 124mg